Contents

BREAK FREE

FROM

ANXIOUS ATTACHMENT

Unlock Your **Stress-Free** Path to Reclaim
Emotional Regulation, Build **Secure**
Relationships, and Enjoy Lasting **Self-Worth**

In Just
15 Minutes
a Day

ANGELINA PECK

Introduction

It's late at night, and you're lying in bed, staring at the ceiling. Your mind races with thoughts: "Did I say something wrong?" "Why hasn't my partner texted me back?" "What if they're losing interest?" This spiral of worry and insecurity is all too familiar. You feel a knot in your stomach as the fear of abandonment creeps in; this is the emotional turmoil of living with anxious attachment.

This book is about understanding and healing from anxious attachment, which is when individuals feel insecure in their romantic or platonic relationships. They often worry about being abandoned or not being enough. It's an exhausting way to live, but don't fret, as there is hope. Addressing this issue is important because it affects how you connect with others and how you see yourself.

I am passionate about this topic because I have firsthand knowledge and experience. This book results from research, personal experience, and a deep commitment to helping others.

Living with anxious attachment can be incredibly challenging. You may struggle with a constant fear of abandonment. Trusting your partner can feel like an impossible task. Fearing your friend may not want to deal with you. Emotional reactions can be intense and overwhelming. These struggles are real, and it's essential to acknowledge them. You're not alone in feeling these emotions.

This book promises to offer you practical strategies, exercises, and tools to manage your anxious attachment. You will learn how to build secure relationships and find lasting self-worth. Through this journey, you will discover ways to heal and grow. The goal is to help you feel better about your situation, feel more secure, and love yourself more.

One of the unique features of this book is its interactive elements. Throughout, you will find journal prompts, exercises, and coloring prompts that will all help you cope with anxiety. These activities are designed to engage you and reinforce the material covered. The book also includes a free downloadable PDF with additional prompts and exercises. These interactive elements will make your journey more engaging and effective.

This book's content is backed by reputable research. It includes insights from therapists and specialists in anxious attachment. The information is well-researched and reliable, and it will provide you with trustworthy guidance on your path to healing.

Throughout the book, you will find affirmations and motivational quotes which are included to provide a positive and supportive experience. They are meant to encourage you and help you feel hopeful. Healing is a journey, and having positive reminders can make a big difference.

The book is structured to guide you through this journey step-by-step. The chapters cover key topics such as understanding anxious attachment, building self-awareness, emotional regulation techniques, and transitioning to secure attachment. Each chapter is designed to provide you with the knowledge and tools you need to heal and grow.

As you read this book, I want you to know you are not alone. Many people, including myself, struggle with anxious attachment, and there is a way to heal. This book guides and supports you every step of the way. You have the strength to overcome these challenges and build the secure, fulfilling relationships you deserve!

So, dear reader, I invite you to embark on this journey of self-discovery and healing. Your path to recovery and lasting self-worth begins here. Let's take the first step together.

"Healing takes courage, and we all have courage, even if we have to dig a little to find it." - Tori Amos

Stop Here! Get your free content!

Below you will find a link to your free
content. Included will be:

...additional prompts

...worksheets

...videos

...coloring pages

...and more!

Free PDF Download!

Sign up at the link below get these
freebies in your inbox.

Simply click the link or scan the QR
code below:

https://angelinapeck.com/le
admagnet

I hope this helps along your journey.
Thank you from the bottom of my heart!
Angelina Peck

CHAPTER ONE

Understanding Anxious Attachment

Y ou're at dinner with your partner, and they seem distracted. Instead of enjoying the meal, your mind starts spinning: "Are they upset with me? Did I do something wrong?" The evening becomes a blur of anxiety and second-guessing. This scene is all too common for those with anxious attachments. It's a relentless cycle of fear and insecurity that can overshadow even the simplest moments of connection.

What is Anxious Attachment?

Anxious attachment is a type of insecure attachment style where individuals often feel insecure and anxious about their relationships. People with this attachment style constantly worry about their partner's feelings and are always on the lookout for signs of abandonment. They need frequent reassurance to feel secure, which can be exhausting for both themselves and their partners. This constant state of anxiety makes it difficult to enjoy relationships fully.

In simpler terms, if you have an anxious attachment style, you might find yourself constantly fearing that your partner will leave you. You might overthink every little interaction, wondering if you've said or done something wrong. This fear of abandonment can lead to behaviors that may seem clingy or overly dependent. You might need continuous validation from your partner or friends to feel secure.

Let's look at Sarah. Sarah is in a loving relationship but can't shake the feeling that her partner might leave her. Every time her partner doesn't respond to a text immediately, she spirals into anxiety, thinking they might be losing interest. She constantly seeks reassurance, asking questions like "Do you still love me?" or "Are you happy with me?" This need for constant validation can strain her relationship, making her partner feel overwhelmed.

Then there's John. John needs continuous validation from his friends and partners. He often feels that he's not good enough and seeks constant approval to feel worthy, which makes him overly dependent on others for his self-esteem, leading to a cycle of anxiety and insecurity.

Critical characteristics of anxious attachment include clinginess and the need for constant reassurance. You might be overthinking and anticipating rejection or abandonment even when there's no real reason to. Trusting your partner can feel like an impossible task despite your deep desire for closeness, creating a paradox where you crave intimacy but push people away with your neediness.

Understanding anxious attachment is crucial for several reasons:

1. It helps you build self-awareness and personal growth. Recognizing your attachment style allows you to understand why you feel and act the way you do in relationships. This awareness is the first step toward change.

2. It can improve your relationship dynamics. By understanding your attachment style, you can communicate your needs more effectively and work on building more secure connections.

3. It reduces emotional distress.

Knowing the root cause of your anxiety can help you manage it better and lead a more fulfilling life.

Understanding anxious attachment is about recognizing the problem and finding ways to heal and grow. This chapter will provide the knowledge and tools to understand your attachment style and begin the journey toward a more secure and fulfilling life.

The Roots of Anxious Attachment: Childhood and Beyond

Imagine a child reaching out for comfort, only to find that sometimes their caregiver is there, and other times, they're not. This inconsistency can leave a lasting mark. Anxious attachment often begins in childhood, shaped by early experiences with primary caregivers. When caregivers are inconsistent—sometimes attentive, sometimes neglectful—the child learns that love and security are unpredictable. Overprotective or overly anxious parents can also contribute to this attachment style. They may hover and respond to every whim, leaving the child incapable of managing emotions independently. Emotional unavailability, where caregivers are physically present but emotionally distant, can make a child feel unseen and unheard, fostering a deep-seated sense of insecurity. As you can see, there are different reasons for developing an anxious attachment.

Significant life events beyond childhood can also influence attachment styles. Traumatic experiences, such as the loss of a loved one, can intensify fears of abandonment and rejection. Relationship breakups can reinforce the belief that love is fleeting and unreliable. Chronic stress or anxiety, whether from personal circumstances or environmental factors, can exacerbate feelings of insecurity and instability. These events can trigger or deepen anxious attachment, making it challenging to form secure, trusting relationships.

Attachment theory provides a framework for understanding these dynamics. John Bowlby, a pioneering attachment theorist, described attachment as a "lasting psychological connectedness between human beings." He believed that early bonds with caregivers shape our ability to form relationships throughout life. Mary Ainsworth expanded on Bowlby's work with her "strange situation" study, identifying three primary attachment styles: secure, anxious-ambivalent (often referred to as anxious attachment), and avoidant. The "secure base" concept is central to attachment theory; it posits that children who feel secure with their caregivers are more likely to explore the world confidently and build healthy relationships.

These early experiences translate into adult behaviors and relationship patterns. Adults with anxious attachment often cling to their partners or friends, fearing that any distance signals will result in abandonment. Trusting others becomes a challenge, as past experiences have taught them that love is conditional and unreliable. This can lead to a cycle of seeking constant reassurance and validation, which can strain relationships and perpetuate feelings of inadequacy.

Understanding the roots of anxious attachment is vital in breaking free from its grip. It allows us to see the connections between past experiences and current behaviors. Recognizing these patterns can help us develop healthier ways of relating to others and ourselves.

Recognizing Anxious Attachment in Your Relationships and How It Affects Them

Anxious attachment can profoundly impact romantic relationships. Imagine being in a relationship where you constantly need reassurance. You repeatedly ask your partner, "Do you still love me?" and continually seek the answer "Yes." This frequent need for validation can strain even the strongest partnerships. Fear of abandonment looms over you, making every disagreement feel like a potential breakup. Trust becomes a significant hurdle, often leading to jealousy and suspicion. You find yourself overthinking every text, every word, every glance. This relentless rumination can create emotional highs and lows, leaving you exhausted and your partner confused.

In these relationships, behavioral patterns emerge that signal anxious attachment. You might find yourself checking your partner's phone or social media, seeking evidence that everything is fine. You ask for constant validation, needing to repeatedly hear "I love you" to feel secure. Interactions and communications are overanalyzed, with every pause or change in tone becoming a source of anxiety. These behaviors can create a cycle of dependency where you rely heavily on your partner for emotional stability, which isn't fair not only to your partner but yourself.

Anxious attachment doesn't just affect romantic relationships; it spills over into friendships and other connections. Maintaining long-term friendships can be challenging as you might feel left out or neglected if friends don't constantly affirm your importance. This can lead to resentment or jealousy, making it hard to sustain these relationships. The need for constant reassurance can be just as draining for friends as for romantic partners. After all, all relationships have a similar foundation with different nuances.

These behaviors place a significant strain on all relationships. Constantly seeking reassurance can make others feel overwhelmed or suffocated, leading them to distance themselves. This, in turn, reinforces your fears of abandonment, creating a vicious cycle of anxiety and dependency. Your relationships become marked by emotional instability, making it hard to build lasting, secure connections.

Consider a scenario where a partner feels suffocated by the constant need for reassurance. Every time they go out with friends, their phone buzzes with messages asking if they still care. This relentless need for validation can drive a wedge between partners, pushing them apart rather than bringing them together. Or a friend feeling neglected by a text that sits unread and is not replied to puts a strain on the friendship. This can lead to misunderstandings and distance, eroding the foundation of the friendship.

To manage these challenges:

1. Start with basic coping strategies.

2. Practice self-soothing techniques like deep breathing or mindfulness to calm your anxiety.

3. Set realistic expectations with your partners and friends; understanding constant reassurance isn't sustainable.

4. Focus on building your self-worth independently so you don't rely solely on others for validation.

If all of these sound overwhelming, don't worry; this book will help you understand each and provide examples.

Recognizing Anxious Attachment in Yourself

To begin recognizing anxious attachment in yourself, you should start with some self-assessment. Ask yourself: Do I frequently worry that my partner will leave me? Do I overanalyze their actions and words, looking for hidden meanings? Do I find it hard to fully enjoy my relationships because I'm always on edge, waiting for something to go wrong? These questions can provide initial insight into your attachment style. Consider using checklists or quizzes to help pinpoint specific behaviors and thoughts indicative of anxious attachment. These tools can guide you in understanding patterns you may not have consciously noticed.

Common signs of anxious attachment are often deeply ingrained in daily life. Persistent fear of abandonment can be a constant companion. You may find yourself overthinking every text, every word, and every glance, which becomes exhausting. This over-analysis often leads to a cycle where you struggle to trust your partner, making it hard to relax and enjoy the relationship. Instead of feeling secure and content, you may spend most of your time worrying about potential problems that might not even exist. This perpetual state of anxiety can overshadow the joy and connection you seek, leaving you feeling isolated even when you're not alone.

Recognizing these patterns is the first step toward healing. Self-awareness is a powerful tool that lays the foundation for personal growth. Understanding your attachment style allows you to identify the root causes of your anxiety and address them directly. This awareness can also enhance your relationship dynamics. When you know why you react a certain way, it becomes easier to communicate your needs and work with your partner to build a more secure bond. Reducing emotional distress creates space for more positive interactions and experiences in your relationships.

Consider the story of a woman who realized her pattern of needing constant reassurance. She noticed that her anxiety spiked whenever her partner didn't immediately respond to her messages. This led her to frequently ask, "Do you still love me?" or "Are you mad at me?" Over time, she recognized how this behavior strained her relationship. By understanding her need for validation, she began to work on building her self-worth independently, leading to a more balanced and fulfilling relationship.

Another example is a man who identified his habit of overthinking. He constantly analyzed his partner's actions, searching for signs of disinterest or rejection. This hyper-vigilance created unnecessary tension. Through self-reflection, he learned to challenge his anxious thoughts and focus on the positive aspects of his relationship, which improved his emotional well-being.

I have done these exact things; I notice a slight change in my husband's mood or reaction to what I ask and wonder, "Is he mad at me?" Working on my self-reflection has made me realize that I am overthinking his facial expressions because I am insecure in the relationship. But this is only the first step. We can dig deeper, and we can heal!

A quote to remember: "You are not to blame for having anxious attachment; it is a result of your past experiences. Recognizing it is a brave step, and you deserve praise for seeking to better yourself." This mindset can help you approach your attachment style with compassion and determination. Understanding anxious attachment in yourself is not about self-criticism; it's about self-discovery and growth. So give yourself some grace.

The Emotional Rollercoaster: Understanding Your Reactions

Living with anxious attachment often feels like riding an emotional rollercoaster. One moment, you experience intense joy and contentment when your partner is attentive and reassuring. The next, you plunge into anxiety and despair at the slightest hint of perceived neglect. During relationship conflicts, this pattern intensifies. Anxiety and fear have you in a tight grip, making it difficult to think clearly or stay calm. When your partner reassures you, relief washes over you like a soothing balm, but this happiness is often short-lived. The cycle of highs and lows can be exhausting, leaving you feeling emotionally drained and overwhelmed. Imagine having to ride a rollercoaster thirty times in a row and the exhaustion you may feel; that's what it may be like.

Common triggers for these reactions are often rooted in everyday interactions. Your partner's unavailability, whether busy at work or needing some time alone, can trigger feelings of neglect and abandonment. Miscommunications or misunderstandings can escalate quickly, turning a minor issue into a significant source of anxiety. A simple example is your partner not responding to a text promptly. This delay can spiral into thoughts of rejection, making you question your relationship's worth and stability. These triggers are often tied to past experiences where love and attention were inconsistent or conditional.

These emotional reactions are deeply connected to past attachment-related experiences. Early childhood experiences, such as inconsistent caregiving or emotional unavailability, lay the groundwork for anxious attachment. Significant life events, like the loss of a loved one or traumatic breakups, can reinforce these patterns. These past experiences shape your current behaviors and emotional responses, making it challenging to break free from the cycle of anxiety and insecurity. Understanding this connection can provide insight into why you react the way you do and highlight areas for growth and healing.

It's helpful to have some coping strategies to manage these intense emotions. Deep breathing exercises can be a quick and effective way to calm your mind and body. When you feel anxiety rising, take a few slow, deep breaths, focusing on the sensation of the air entering and leaving your lungs. Journaling about triggers and responses can also be beneficial. Take some time each day to write about what triggered your anxiety and how you reacted. Reflect on these entries to identify patterns and develop new ways to respond. These initial strategies can help you gain control over your emotional reactions and create a more stable and fulfilling relationship dynamic.

Real-Life Examples of Anxious Attachment

Consider the case of Emily, who has been in a long-term relationship for five years. Emily's anxious attachment is a constant fear that her partner, Ryan, will leave her. Emily panics whenever Ryan comes home late or doesn't respond to her texts immediately. She calls repeatedly, sends multiple messages, and imagines worst-case scenarios. This behavior has led to numerous arguments, with Ryan feeling overwhelmed and Emily feeling even more insecure. Without intervention, this pattern can lead to emotional burnout for both partners, straining the relationship to the breaking point. Emily's constant need for reassurance and Ryan's feeling of suffocation create a cycle that is hard to break.

In another scenario, consider Jake, who struggles with anxious attachment in multiple friendships. He always feels like he's on the outskirts of his friend group, worrying that he's not included or valued. When his friends make plans without him, Jake feels devastated. He often sends long messages seeking validation, asking if he's done something wrong. Over time, his friends find his neediness exhausting, leading to a gradual distancing. Jake's fear of being left out becomes a self-fulfilling prophecy as his friends pull away to avoid the constant emotional demands. This isolation exacerbates his anxiety, creating a vicious cycle of dependency and rejection.

Without addressing anxious attachment, the consequences can be severe. Relationship breakdowns are common, as partners and friends struggle to cope with the constant need for validation and the emotional highs and lows. Emotional burnout becomes a real risk, with the individual and their loved ones feeling drained. The impact on mental health is significant, with increased anxiety, depression, and a pervasive sense of unworthiness.

However, there is hope. Take the example of Mark and Lisa, a couple who managed to work through anxious attachment issues together. Mark struggled with feeling insecure and constantly needed reassurance. With understanding and patience, Lisa encouraged open communication and sought therapy with Mark. Through consistent effort and mutual support, Mark learned to manage his anxieties, and Lisa learned to provide reassurance healthily. Their relationship strengthened, and Mark transitioned to a more secure attachment style.

Similarly, consider Anna, who managed to transition from an anxious attachment to a secure attachment style. She sought therapy, practiced self-awareness, and engaged in mindfulness exercises. Over time, Anna learned to trust herself and her relationships, reducing her need for constant reassurance. Her friendships and romantic relationships flourished as she became more confident and less anxious. This transformation was not overnight, but with dedication and support, she achieved a level of emotional stability she had never thought possible.

These stories highlight the challenges and triumphs of dealing with anxious attachment. They show that while the road may be difficult, change is possible. With the right tools and support, it is possible to move from a place of insecurity to one of confidence and security.

At this point, I hope the belief and realization that there is a brighter future than feeling this way is coursing through you. I have had to adjust to ensure I don't drive a wedge in my relationships or friendships. We will do this together.

Common Myths and Misconceptions About Anxious Attachment

One common myth about anxious attachment is that it means you are weak or needy. This misconception can be incredibly damaging, making individuals feel ashamed or embarrassed about their emotional needs and maybe wanting to hide away from them. The truth is anxious attachment is not a sign of weakness but a response to inconsistent care and emotional neglect. It's a way the brain has learned to protect itself from perceived threats. Society often stigmatizes emotional vulnerability, labeling it as neediness. But seeking connection and reassurance is a natural human desire. Understanding this can help dismantle the shame associated with anxious attachment.

Another pervasive myth is that anxious attachment cannot be changed. This belief can lead to hopelessness and resignation, making individuals feel trapped in their anxiety. In reality, attachment styles are malleable. Research shows individuals can move toward a more secure attachment style with consistent effort, therapy, and supportive relationships. Studies have demonstrated that attachment behaviors can be modified through interventions like Cognitive Behavioral Therapy (CBT) and mindfulness practices. This evidence offers hope and a path forward for those feeling stuck.

A third myth is that only women experience anxious attachment. This stereotype is rooted in outdated gender norms that portray women as more emotional and men as more stoic. However, anxious attachment affects individuals regardless of gender. Studies indicate that both men and women can develop this attachment style due to similar childhood experiences and environmental factors. By recognizing that anxious attachment is not gender-specific, we can better support everyone who struggles with it.

These myths persist due to societal stigma around mental health and a misunderstanding of attachment theory. Emotional struggles are often dismissed or misunderstood, leading to harmful stereotypes. Additionally, many people are unfamiliar with the concepts of attachment theory, which can perpetuate these misconceptions. Educating ourselves and others can challenge these myths and promote a more compassionate understanding of anxious attachment.

The biological basis of attachment styles further debunks these myths. The amygdala, a part of the brain involved in emotional processing, plays a significant role in responding to perceived threats in relationships. Hormones like oxytocin and cortisol also influence attachment behaviors. Oxytocin, often called the "love hormone," promotes bonding and trust, while cortisol, the stress hormone, can heighten anxiety. Understanding these biological factors can help shed light on anxious attachment and reinforce that it is a natural, though challenging, response to one's environment.

Psychological research provides additional insight. Mary Ainsworth's "Strange Situation" experiment and the Adult Attachment Interview (AAI) have shown how attachment styles develop and manifest. These studies underscore that attachment behaviors are learned and can be unlearned with the proper support and strategies. This knowledge empowers individuals to take proactive steps toward healing.

Embracing a positive and proactive mindset is crucial. Understanding and managing anxious attachment is not a path of self-criticism but growth and healing. Overcoming these misconceptions can lead to a healthier self-view and better relationships. Recognizing that change is possible opens up new possibilities for personal and relational fulfillment.

Addressing these myths can help us develop a more accurate and compassionate understanding of anxious attachment. This knowledge empowers individuals and creates more supportive and empathetic relationships.

> *"Our sorrows and wounds are healed only when we touch them with compassion."*
>
> Jack Kornfield

CHAPTER TWO

The Emotional Journey

"We are stronger, gentler, more resilient, and more beautiful than any of us imagine."

Mark Nepo

Managing Intense Emotional Reactions

You're at a family gathering, and suddenly, you're overwhelmed by a wave of emotions. You're not sure what triggered it, but the feeling is unmistakable—anxiety, fear, an urgent need for reassurance. These intense emotional reactions are common for those with an anxious attachment and can be bewildering. Your nervous system, finely tuned to sense danger, reacts as if under constant threat, often leading to emotional outbursts or hypersensitivity.

Understanding why these reactions occur is the first step toward managing them. Your body and mind respond to cues that remind them of past wounds, even if the present situation doesn't warrant such a response. This connection between past and present is why emotional regulation becomes crucial. Learning to soothe yourself can transform how you experience these moments. Deep-breathing exercises, for instance, activate the parasympathetic nervous system, calming the mind and reducing stress hormones. By focusing on the breath, you anchor yourself in the present, creating a buffer against overwhelming emotions.

Grounding techniques are equally effective. They help you stay present by redirecting your focus to the physical world around you. Notice the texture of the chair you're sitting on, the sounds in the room, or the sensation of your feet on the ground. These simple actions can pull you out of your mind's whirlwind and back into reality. Physical activity also plays a vital role in emotional regulation. Exercise is an outlet for pent-up energy and anxiety, releasing endorphins that elevate mood and foster a sense of well-being.

Emotional triggers are the cues that set off these intense reactions. They are often linked to past experiences and can be as varied as a partner's silence, a change in plans, or unmet expectations. For those with anxious attachment, a partner's lack of communication might be perceived as a prelude to rejection. A slight change in routine could trigger fears of abandonment. These triggers are deeply personal, shaped by the unique tapestry of your life experiences.

Recognizing your emotional triggers is empowering. It allows you to anticipate and prepare for situations that might provoke anxiety. Keeping an emotional trigger journal can be an invaluable tool. By documenting situations that lead to intense emotional reactions, you can begin to identify patterns and gain insight into your emotional landscape. Keeping an emotional trigger journal is not meant to be degrading. Remember as you write that this is a tool to help you move forward. Don't criticize the trigger; identify it to help with pattern recognition. Reflective practices, such as mindfulness, further enhance this awareness. Regularly engaging in mindfulness exercises, you train yourself to notice triggers in real time, allowing you to respond with intention rather than reflex.

Interactive Exercise: Emotional Trigger Journal

Start by creating a dedicated journal for tracking your emotional triggers. Note the date, time, and situation each time you experience an intense emotional reaction. Describe your feelings and any thoughts that accompanied them. Over time, look for patterns—are there common themes or situations that consistently provoke anxiety? Use this awareness to develop strategies for managing these triggers, such as preparing yourself mentally for anticipated stressors or practicing grounding techniques beforehand.

By understanding and managing your emotional reactions, you not only navigate your relationships more smoothly but also cultivate a more profound sense of self-awareness and control.

Coping with Chronic Anxiety in Relationships

A common characteristic of having an anxious attachment in a relationship is chronic anxiety, which often is fueled by deep-seated fears of rejection and abandonment. This anxiety can feel like a constant nag, influencing how you perceive your partner's actions and behaviors. You might find yourself hypervigilant, scanning for any sign—real or imagined—that something is "wrong." A change in tone, a missed call, or even an ambiguous text can trigger a tsunami of anxious thoughts, leaving you feeling on edge and insecure. This perpetual state of alertness is exhausting for you and your partner, who may feel the pressure to reassure you constantly.

Managing this anxiety requires practical strategies that address both the mind and body. Relaxation techniques, such as progressive muscle relaxation, can be incredibly effective. Focusing on tensing and releasing different muscle groups can calm your nervous system and reduce physical tension. Cognitive restructuring is another powerful tool; it involves identifying and challenging the negative thoughts that fuel your anxiety. You can reduce their emotional impact by reframing these thoughts to be more balanced and realistic. For example, if you think, "They didn't text back because they're mad at me," try reframing it to, "They might be busy and will respond when they can."

Creating emotional safety in your relationship is also crucial. Emotional safety means living in an environment where both partners feel secure in expressing themselves without fear of judgment or retaliation. The safe feeling we all crave can be achieved with a foundation of open and honest communication. Encourage discussions about each other's needs, fears, and expectations. Setting mutual boundaries can also help define acceptable and unacceptable, providing a framework for healthy interactions. When both partners agree on these boundaries, it reduces ambiguity and minimizes misunderstandings, making the relationship feel more stable and predictable.

Real-life examples can illuminate how these strategies work in practice. Consider a couple who implemented regular "check-ins" to develop and maintain emotional safety. Every Sunday evening, they sit down and discuss their feelings and any issues that arise during the week. This consistency allows them to address concerns before they escalate, reinforcing their emotional bond and reducing anxiety. Another individual found solace in journaling to process their relationship anxiety. By writing down their thoughts and feelings, they could gain perspective and clarity, making it easier to communicate their needs to their partner. An important step not to leave out when journaling is to convey what you've discovered through journaling with your partner.

Interactive Element: Journaling Prompt

Reflect on a recent moment when you felt anxious in your relationship. What were the specific thoughts and feelings you experienced? Write them down, and then try to challenge negative or anxious thoughts by considering alternative explanations. How might you communicate these feelings to your partner to create understanding and emotional safety? How can you stay calm and open to their response and genuinely believe and hear what they say?

These approaches not only help manage chronic anxiety but also pave the way for more secure and fulfilling relationships. The key lies in recognizing the patterns that contribute to anxiety and taking proactive steps to address them. Through consistent practice and open communication, you can transform your relationship into a safe haven where you and your partner can thrive.

Overthinking and Rumination

Overthinking and rumination can feel like an endless loop of thoughts. Although these concepts are often used interchangeably, they have distinct meanings. Overthinking involves excessively dwelling on a problem or situation, leading to analysis paralysis. It keeps you stuck in a cycle of evaluating every possible outcome, which can be mentally exhausting. Rumination, on the other hand, is the repetitive focus on distressing thoughts and events. It is less about solving a problem and more about obsessing over it, feeding anxiety and insecurity. This habit of ruminating feeds into your anxiety, which in turn allows your negative beliefs about yourself or the relationship to be reinforced. The mind gets trapped in a cycle where worries are magnified, and solutions seem impossible to achieve.

The impact of overthinking on daily life and relationships can be significant. You might lie awake at night, unable to turn off your thoughts. Laying in bed and being unable to sleep becomes the norm as you replay conversations, analyze interactions, and predict unfavorable outcomes. This mental chatter can lead to misunderstandings with loved ones. When caught up in your thoughts, it's easy to misinterpret a partner's silence as disinterest or a friend's delay in texting back as rejection. These assumptions can create unnecessary tension and conflict, straining your cherished bonds. The constant mental noise can also affect your ability to be present, making it challenging to enjoy moments of connection and joy. Over time, this can wear down your mental resilience and leave you feeling isolated, even if loved ones surround you.

Breaking the cycle of overthinking requires deliberate effort and practical strategies. One effective approach is setting designated "worry times." Allocate a specific time each day to focus on your concerns. When anxious thoughts arise outside this window, remind yourself that you'll address them later. This containment strategy helps prevent worries from spilling into every aspect of your life. One thing to ensure is you don't skip the worry time and let everything bottle up. Practicing mindfulness also plays a crucial role in reducing rumination. By staying grounded in the present moment, you can break free from the grip of repetitive thoughts. Mindfulness techniques, such as focusing on your breath or observing your surroundings, anchor you in the here and now. Activities that distract the mind, like hobbies or exercise, can also provide relief. These pursuits offer a break from mental rumination and allow your mind to realize the sense of accomplishment and joy it can feel.

Success stories offer hope and guidance for overcoming overthinking. Take, for example, someone who found solace in using mindfulness apps. By incorporating guided meditations and mindfulness practices into their daily routine, they were able to reduce rumination and cultivate a sense of calm. Another person turned to cognitive-behavioral techniques to challenge their anxious thoughts. By identifying and reframing negative beliefs, they gained control over their mental patterns and experienced relief from the constant cycle of overthinking. These stories highlight the potential for change and the power of practical strategies to transform how you relate to your thoughts. Remember, you are not alone in these scenarios. Many, including myself, have walked this path and found peace, proving that with effort and support, you, too, can quiet the storm of overthinking.

"We have anxious thoughts because the brain is trying to keep us alive. To the brain, survival is much more important than happiness. So, the brain often conjures up worst case scenarios and "what ifs", so that we can prepare for disaster. The trouble is, the brain regularly gets it wrong."

Dr. Lucy Russell, Clinical Psychologist

The Fear of Abandonment

Fear of abandonment is like a shadow that follows you, darkening your interactions and relationships. It's an all-encompassing dread that those you care about will leave, physically or emotionally, leaving you feeling alone and unworthy. This fear is pervasive in those with an anxious attachment, deeply rooted in early experiences where love felt conditional or inconsistent. If your childhood was marked by caregivers who were emotionally distant or unpredictable, you likely internalized the belief that affection and stability could vanish at any moment. These early lessons taught your nervous system to remain on high alert, a survival mechanism that now translates into an adult life filled with anxiety and hypervigilance. This fear doesn't just vanish with age; instead, it can become more pronounced with each new experience of rejection or perceived abandonment, reinforcing the cycle of anxiety.

In relationships, this fear manifests as a relentless need for reassurance. You might find yourself constantly seeking validation from your partner, needing to hear "I love you" or "I'm not leaving" to calm the overwhelming insecurity within. Yet, this desire for reassurance can become a double-edged sword. Partners might misinterpret your neediness as distrust or dependency, leading to tension and misunderstanding. Every action or inaction by your partner can be misread as a sign of impending abandonment. A missed call, a delayed text, or a quiet evening can spiral into a narrative of rejection, causing you to react with desperation or withdrawal. This cycle of fear and reassurance-seeking can strain relationships, pushing partners away even as you try to pull them closer. It's a painful paradox: the more you crave closeness, the more your fear-driven behaviors can create distance.

Cognitive-behavioral strategies can be transformative in managing fear. Start by challenging negative thoughts that fuel your anxiety. When the fear of abandonment rears its ugly head, ask yourself: "Is this thought based on reality, or is it a projection of past wounds?" Visualization exercises can also help build a sense of security. Close your eyes and imagine a place where you feel safe and loved. Picture the details—the colors, the sounds, the sensations. This mental refuge can become a powerful tool in calming your mind when fears of abandonment arise. These techniques help rewire your thought process, gradually breaking the cycle of fear and reaction.

Consider my story: I grappled with an overwhelming fear of abandonment. Therapy became my lifeline, providing a space to unpack my past and understand how it shaped my present worries. I was given excellent advice to communicate with my husband and let him know when this fear arose. At first, I wasn't sure what triggered the flood of emotion, but through consistent work, I learned to trust myself and my husband, reducing my need for constant reassurance. Then there's Alex and Jordan, a couple who found themselves in a cycle of misunderstanding fueled by Alex's fear of abandonment. They decided to work together, attending couples therapy to build trust and communication. By sharing their vulnerabilities and setting clear boundaries, they created a foundation of trust that allowed Alex to feel secure without needing constant validation. These stories testify to the power of intentional effort and support in overcoming the fear of abandonment.

How Anxious Attachment Affects Your Self-Worth

Living with anxious attachment often feels like being on unstable ground, where your sense of self-worth gets chipped away with every relationship shift. People with this attachment style frequently struggle with low self-esteem. When love or affection is unpredictable early in life, children internalize the belief that their worth is conditional, dependent on external validation and approval. These early experiences plant seeds of doubt, making rejections and failures feel like confirmations of inadequacy. Over time, the need for constant reassurance becomes a coping mechanism, a way to momentarily silence the relentless self-doubt and insecurity that echo in the mind.

The cycle of low self-esteem and anxious attachment feeds on itself, creating a loop that is hard to break. Negative self-talk becomes a constant companion, whispering doubts and fears that erode confidence. Seeking reassurance often backfires, as the temporary relief it provides is overshadowed by the underlying belief that love and acceptance are fleeting. Each time you depend on others for validation, you reinforce the idea that you are not enough on your own, perpetuating a cycle that drains your self-worth even further.

During a session, my therapist and I decided to name the negative voice in my head that was talking bad about me. I called her my critical voice, and she constantly fueled my fear of not being enough. Giving the voice its own name allowed me to detach myself from this voice and say, "Shut up, that's not true," when these thoughts started to creep in. Doing this has been a great help with knowing that the voice is just my insecurity speaking, and I can break the cycle by not listening.

Breaking free from this cycle begins with self-acceptance. Embracing who you are, flaws and all is a powerful antidote to the corrosive effects of low self-esteem. Practicing self-compassion exercises can be transformative. By treating yourself with the same kindness and understanding you'd offer a friend, you can begin to heal. Reflecting on personal strengths and achievements is also crucial. Take time to acknowledge your successes and the qualities that make you unique. This reflection can help shift your focus from perceived shortcomings to genuine accomplishments, allowing a more balanced self-view.

Consider the story of Laura, who struggled with self-worth after years of seeking validation from others. She began using daily affirmations, repeating positive statements about herself each morning. Over time, these affirmations became ingrained, gradually replacing the negative self-talk that had dominated her thoughts. This example highlights the power of intentional actions in reshaping self-perception.

This chapter has explored the intricate relationship between anxious attachment and self-worth, uncovering the roots and consequences of low self-esteem. Understanding this connection is a vital step toward healing. By nourishing self-acceptance and breaking the cycle of dependency on external validation, you can cultivate a resilient and enduring sense of self-worth. In the next chapter, we'll dive into practical exercises and strategies to further support this transformative process.

> *"Empathy has no script. There is no right way or wrong way to do it. It's simply listening, holding space, withholding judgment, emotionally connecting, and communicating that incredibly healing message of 'You're not alone.'"*
>
> Brené Brown

CHAPTER THREE

Building Self-Awareness and Acceptance

The Power of Self-Awareness

T hink about standing before a mirror, not just seeing your reflection but genuinely understanding the layers beneath it. This is the essence of self-awareness—a journey into your mind to uncover the thoughts and emotions that shape your behaviors and decisions. When you cultivate self-awareness, you gain the ability to recognize your internal landscape. This means understanding the ebb and flow of your emotions and how they influence your actions. For many, this newfound clarity becomes a powerful tool for navigating life's complexities. It allows you to step back and observe how certain feelings drive your responses, helping you break free from automatic reactions that may not serve your best interests.

Self-awareness is not just about introspection; it's about transformation. With increased self-awareness, you can regulate your emotions more effectively, making staying calm in the face of stress or conflict easier. It also enhances decision-making as you become more attuned to what truly matters. This clarity reduces impulsivity, allowing you to make choices aligned with your values and long-term goals. Furthermore, self-awareness improves relationships. By understanding your needs and triggers, you communicate more clearly and empathetically, creating deeper connections with others. This understanding creates a space for mutual respect and trust to flourish, paving the way for more authentic and fulfilling interactions.

Several practices can be profoundly beneficial in enhancing self-awareness. Mindfulness meditation is a cornerstone technique that lets you focus on the present moment without judgment. Regularly engaging in mindfulness makes you more aware of your thoughts and feelings as they arise, allowing you to respond rather than react. Daily reflection practices, such as setting aside a few minutes each evening to review your day, help you identify patterns in your emotions and behaviors. Keeping a self-awareness journal can also be transformative. By writing about your thoughts and feelings, you gain insights into your inner world, uncovering recurring themes and beliefs that guide your actions. This journaling practice creates a dialogue with yourself, allowing you to peel back the layers and appreciate a deeper understanding and acceptance of who you are.

Interactive Exercise: Mindfulness Meditation Practice

Set aside ten minutes each day for a simple mindfulness meditation. Find a quiet space and sit comfortably. Close your eyes and focus on your breath. Notice each inhale and exhale, allowing thoughts to pass without judgment. If your mind wanders, gently bring your focus back to your breath. This practice helps ground you in the present moment, enhancing your awareness of your inner state.

As you embrace self-awareness, you open the door to personal growth and relational harmony. This awareness empowers you to navigate life with intention and clarity, forging a path toward a more fulfilling and authentic existence. This will allow you to continue on the path to learning how to break free from the anxious attachment—building that foundation to a better you.

The Role of Self-Compassion in Healing

Imagine treating yourself with the same kindness and understanding you offer a dear friend. This is the essence of self-compassion—an approach to life that acknowledges your humanity, flaws, and all. Self-compassion empowers you, unlike self-pity, which can lead to a spiral of helplessness and victimhood. It involves recognizing that everyone makes mistakes and has shortcomings. By embracing this perspective, you can create a nurturing inner environment where growth and healing are possible. When you practice self-compassion, you allow yourself to be imperfect, stumble, and learn without harsh judgment or criticism.

For individuals with anxious attachment, self-compassion is a powerful tool for emotional healing. It reduces anxiety and stress by providing a buffer against the harsh self-criticism that often accompanies anxious thoughts. This practice builds emotional resilience, enabling you to bounce back more readily from setbacks and challenges. As you treat yourself with kindness, your self-esteem naturally improves. You begin to see yourself as worthy of love and respect, independent of external validation. This shift in perspective can transform your interactions with others, leading to healthier relationships built on mutual understanding and acceptance.

Despite its benefits, practicing self-compassion presents challenges. Many struggle with internalized criticism and self-judgment, ingrained patterns that make self-kindness feel foreign. You might fear that being gentle with yourself equates to weakness or indulgence. These barriers can deter you from embracing self-compassion fully. However, recognizing these obstacles is the first step toward overcoming them. By understanding that self-compassion is not about excusing bad behavior but about learning to create a supportive inner dialogue, you can begin to dismantle these barriers and embrace a healthier mindset.

Consider the "Golden Rule" as most know it, but it's also from Luke 6:31, "Do to others as you would have them do to you." This is saying to treat others as you would want to be treated. Now, think about the way you may speak to yourself or the way you treat yourself. Would you want to be treated that way by someone else? I'm assuming the answer is no because, knowing how I can talk bad about myself, I would be heartbroken to hear those words from someone else. Learning to treat and empathize with ourselves as if we were our best friends is incredibly healing.

To cultivate self-compassion, consider incorporating mindful self-compassion meditation into your routine. This practice encourages you to observe your thoughts and feelings without judgment and introduces you to gentle awareness. Self-forgiveness is another crucial aspect. When you make a mistake, instead of criticizing yourself, acknowledge the error and gently remind yourself that mistakes are a natural part of life. Writing compassionate letters to yourself can also be therapeutic. In these letters, express understanding and support for your struggles, just as you would a friend. Practicing self-compassionate language is vital, too. Replace harsh self-talk with affirmations of kindness and encouragement, gradually reprogramming your inner dialogue.

Incorporating self-compassion into daily life can be transformative. After making a mistake, speak to yourself kindly instead of dwelling on it. Remember that it's okay to err and that growth often stems from these moments. Allow yourself to take breaks and rest without guilt, recognizing that rest is essential to self-care. Celebrate small achievements, no matter how minor they may seem. These acknowledgments reinforce your self-worth and build a foundation of positivity and resilience. As you practice self-compassion, you likely notice shifts in how you perceive yourself and interact with others, creating a ripple effect of kindness and understanding in your life.

Interactive Element: Self-Compassionate Language Exercise

Take a moment to reflect on a recent mistake or challenge. Write down the self-critical thoughts that arose. Then, rewrite these thoughts using compassionate language. For example, if your initial thought was, "I can't believe I messed up again," reframe it as, "It's okay to make mistakes; I'm learning and growing." Keep this exercise handy and revisit it whenever self-criticism surfaces, gradually shifting your internal dialogue toward compassion.

> *"You've been criticizing yourself for years and it hasn't worked. Try approving of yourself and see what happens."*
>
> Louise Hay

Affirmations to Build Self-Worth

A small but powerful tool at your disposal that can transform how you see yourself and the world around you. This is the power of affirmations—positive statements crafted to challenge and overcome negative thoughts that often plague our minds. At their core, affirmations are about reinforcing positive self-beliefs. They are gentle reminders that you are enough, worthy of love and respect, and capable of navigating life's complexities. You reshape your internal dialogue by consistently repeating these affirmations, gradually silencing the critical voice that undermines your self-worth.

The impact of affirmations on emotional health and self-esteem can be profound. Regularly engaging with affirmations can significantly improve your mood and outlook on life. They provide a beacon of positivity, helping to lift you out of the fog of negativity that anxious attachment often creates. With each repetition, your confidence grows, gradually replacing the seeds of doubt with a sense of self-assuredness. Over time, affirmations can reduce negative self-talk, which often acts like a persistent background noise, eroding your self-esteem. Instead of focusing on perceived shortcomings, you start to see and appreciate your strengths, leading to a more balanced and healthy self-view.

Creating personalized affirmations is an empowering process. It begins with identifying the negative beliefs that you wish to counteract. Take a moment to reflect on the thoughts that frequently undermine your self-worth. Perhaps you often think, "I'm not good enough," or "I always mess things up." Once these beliefs are identified, you can craft specific, positive statements that directly challenge them. For example, if you struggle with self-love and acceptance, an affirmation like "I am worthy of love and respect" can be a powerful counterbalance. If confidence is an issue, try affirmations such as "I trust my ability to navigate relationships." For those grappling with anxiety, "I am enough just as I am" can offer solace and reassurance.

Incorporating affirmations into your daily routine is a simple yet effective strategy. Consider starting your day by repeating affirmations during your morning routine. Whether spoken aloud or silently to yourself, these words set a positive tone for the day. Writing affirmations in a journal can also be a meaningful practice, allowing you to reflect on their significance and how they shape your mindset. Writing affirmations on sticky notes and placing them around your home is also helpful. Seeing these daily reminders can reinforce their message, gradually shifting your thoughts toward positivity. Additionally, various apps and recordings offer affirmation practices you can listen to, providing a convenient way to engage with them.

It is most powerful to write it out or print it on nice paper and stick it around me where I know I'll see it. I also will say them aloud. This is more powerful for me and allows me to combat those negative thoughts that immediately arise. A couple of affirmations I have around my room say, "I don't need to be perfect. I just need to try my best," and the other one says, "It's okay, I'm okay, We're okay."

Interactive Element: Affirmation Creation Exercise

Take a moment to think about a negative belief you hold about yourself. Write it down, then craft an affirmation that directly challenges this belief. For example, if your negative thought is "I can't handle conflict," your affirmation might be "I approach challenges calmly and confidently." Repeat this affirmation daily, integrating it into your routine to help rewire your thought patterns.

Through these practices, affirmations become more than words; they become a lifeline to a more positive and empowered you. As you integrate these practices into your life, you likely notice a shift in how you perceive yourself and interact with the world. Affirmations are not about denying challenges or pretending everything is perfect; they're about acknowledging your worth and potential, even in the face of difficulties.

Journaling for Self-Discovery

Journaling is like having a conversation with yourself. It offers a space to lay out your thoughts and emotions, letting you explore and understand them without judgment. This practice is beneficial for managing anxious attachment, as it promotes self-discovery and emotional regulation. Putting pen to paper enhances your self-awareness, slowly uncovering the patterns and triggers that influence your behavior. It becomes a refuge where you can safely delve into your inner world, making sense of the chaos that reigns there. In this process of reflection, journaling helps you process emotions that might otherwise remain bottled up, providing clarity and insight that can lead to meaningful change.

There are several journaling practices that can cater to different needs and preferences. Free writing is one such method, where you allow your thoughts to flow unfiltered onto the page. This can be liberating, as it frees you from the constraints of structure and expectation, letting your subconscious thoughts emerge naturally. Prompt-based journaling, on the other hand, offers direction by providing specific questions or themes to explore. These prompts can guide your reflections, helping you focus on particular aspects of your life or experiences. Gratitude journals are another option, encouraging you to note things you are thankful for daily. By shifting your focus to the positive, you cultivate an attitude of appreciation and contentment. Reflective journaling, meanwhile, involves looking back on past experiences to draw lessons and insights. This method can help you identify recurring patterns, allowing you to understand how your past shapes your present.

Here are some prompts to consider to assist you in your journaling journey. Reflect on a recent situation where you felt anxious. What thoughts and feelings did you experience? This prompt can help you unpack the emotions that accompany anxiety, allowing you to see them in a new light. Another prompt could be to write about a time when you felt secure and loved. What made that experience different? By recalling positive experiences, you can identify the elements contributing to emotional security, helping you seek out and cultivate them. Consider listing three things you can do to practice self-compassion today. This exercise encourages actionable self-care, reminding you of the importance of kindness towards yourself. Lastly, reflect on a recent interaction with a loved one. How did your attachment style influence your response? This prompt helps you connect your behavior to your attachment style, promoting greater self-awareness and growth.

Incorporating journaling into your daily routine can make it a consistent and beneficial habit. Set aside dedicated time each day, even if it's just a few minutes, to engage in this reflective practice. This creates a routine that signals your mind that it's time for introspection. Creating a comfortable journaling space can enhance this experience, making it a sanctuary where you feel at ease to explore your thoughts. Whether you prefer a digital or physical journal, choose a format that best suits your needs and lifestyle. Some people find the tactile sensation of writing by hand grounding, while others appreciate the convenience of digital journaling. Ultimately, the goal is to create a habit that fits seamlessly into your life, providing a regular opportunity for reflection and growth.

As you conclude this chapter on building self-awareness and acceptance, remember these practices are stepping stones toward more profound understanding and healing. Journaling, self-compassion, and affirmations empower you to connect with yourself more authentically. As you turn the page, prepare to explore the practical exercises and strategies that will further support your path to emotional resilience and secure relationships.

CHAPTER FOUR

Practical Exercises and Strategies for Healing

"Sometimes you can't calm the storm, so it's best to stop trying. What you can do is calm yourself. The storm will pass."

Timber Hawkeye

The Importance of Emotional Regulation

Y ou're sitting in traffic, and suddenly, a wave of anxiety hits you. Your heart races, thoughts scatter, and you feel an overwhelming urge to escape. This scenario highlights the importance of emotional regulation. Emotional regulation is the ability to manage and respond to emotional experiences healthily. While it might sound straightforward, mastering it can be transformative, especially for those with anxious attachment. Differentiating between emotional suppression and regulation is critical. Suppression involves pushing emotions away, often leading to increased stress and anxiety. In contrast, regulation is about acknowledging, understanding, and managing emotions constructively. Emotional regulation enables you to process your feelings without becoming overwhelmed, paving the way for more balanced and fulfilling interactions.

Effective emotional regulation offers numerous benefits. It can significantly improve mental health by reducing anxiety and stress. When you can navigate your emotions skillfully, you experience fewer emotional outbursts and more stability. This stability enhances relationship satisfaction, as you can better communicate your needs and understand your partner's perspectives. Additionally, emotional regulation improves decision-making under stress. Instead of reacting impulsively, you can pause, consider your options, and choose a response that aligns with your values and goals. This mindful approach benefits your mental well-being and allows you to have healthier relationships and make great life choices.

Conversely, poor emotional regulation can lead to significant downsides. Without it, you may be ensnared in frequent relationship conflicts and misunderstandings. Mismanaged emotions can escalate minor disagreements into major disputes, creating a cycle of tension and resentment. Higher levels of stress and anxiety are also expected consequences. When emotions are left unchecked, they can wreak havoc on your mental and physical health. Think about a bottle of any carbonated drink; the more you shake, it relates to holding those emotions in, and eventually opening it will cause a huge mess. Chronic stress can lead to a host of health issues, from insomnia to heart problems. As you can see, this highlights the importance of developing effective emotional regulation skills as a foundation for a healthier, more balanced life.

Emotional dysregulation is a hallmark of anxious attachment, often exacerbating feelings of insecurity and inadequacy. Individuals with anxious attachment may struggle to manage their emotions, leading to intense reactions that can strain relationships. Learning emotional regulation skills is crucial for healing and building secure connections. By developing these skills, you can break free from the cycle of anxiety and create more stable, fulfilling relationships. This process involves retraining your brain to respond to emotional triggers in healthier ways, strengthening resilience and confidence.

Several practical techniques can be invaluable in cultivating emotional regulation. Deep breathing exercises are a simple yet powerful way to calm the mind and body. Focusing on your breath can anchor you in the present moment, reducing anxiety and promoting relaxation. Progressive muscle relaxation is another effective method. It involves systematically tensing and releasing different muscle groups, helping to relieve physical tension and stress. Cognitive restructuring is a cognitive-behavioral technique that encourages you to challenge and reframe negative thoughts. By identifying unhelpful thought patterns and replacing them with more balanced perspectives, you can reduce their emotional impact and benefit from a more positive outlook. When practiced consistently, these techniques can transform how you navigate emotions, leading to a more balanced and fulfilling life.

Deep-Breathing Techniques for Instant Calm

Picture this: you're in a tense situation, and your heart is pounding. Your nervous system is in overdrive, triggering your fight-or-flight response. Deep breathing can be your lifeline in these moments. It works by activating the parasympathetic nervous system, which calms the body. Engaging in deep breathing signals your body to relax, reducing cortisol and other stress hormones. This physiological shift can transform a state of panic into calm, allowing you to approach situations with clarity and composure.

One of the most straightforward deep breathing techniques is diaphragmatic breathing. Begin by sitting comfortably. Place one hand on your chest and the other on your abdomen. Inhale deeply through your nose, allowing your abdomen to expand while keeping your chest still. Exhale slowly through your mouth. Another method is box breathing, where you inhale for a count of four, hold the breath for four, exhale for four, and pause for four before repeating. The 4-7-8 breathing technique involves inhaling for four seconds, holding the breath for seven, and exhaling for eight. Each method provides a structure that guides your breath, making it easier to focus and relax. Try out these techniques for yourself and see which suits you better. I am a fan of box breathing, as I have heard many soldiers use this technique to ease their minds.

It works wonders for me when I am having an anxiety attack. Whichever one works for you is the best option; there is no one "right" way.

There are countless opportunities to incorporate these breathing techniques into your daily life. Before a stressful meeting or conversation, take a few moments to practice deep breathing. This can center you, reduce anxiety, and prepare you to engage more effectively. During moments of stress in relationships, whether it's a disagreement or an uncomfortable silence, pausing to breathe deeply can help you respond with empathy and understanding rather than react out of fear. Consider incorporating deep breathing into your morning or bedtime routine as a daily relaxation practice. This consistent practice can foster a sense of calm and stability, even amid life's challenges. I do my deep breathing right before bed as it allows my mind to calm down for the night.

Try setting reminders throughout the day to make deep breathing a regular habit. Use your phone or a sticky note on your desk as a gentle nudge to pause and breathe. Incorporating breathing exercises into established routines can also help. For instance, pair a few minutes of deep breathing with your morning coffee or during your evening wind-down. By integrating these techniques into your daily life, you create a foundation of calm that supports emotional resilience and well-being.

Grounding Methods to Stay Present

Feeling untethered, as if a strong wind could blow you away at any moment, can make you highly anxious. Grounding techniques are here to anchor you, pulling focus back to the present when anxiety threatens to overwhelm you. These methods connect you with your immediate environment, drawing attention away from racing thoughts and into the tangible world around you. By engaging your senses and physicality, grounding helps break the cycle of anxiety, fostering a sense of calm and stability. It's about shifting your mental state from the abstract and overwhelming to the concrete and manageable, allowing your mind to rest and recover.

The 5-4-3-2-1 technique is a popular grounding exercise that involves identifying five things you can see, four you can touch, three you can hear, two you can smell, and one you can taste. This exercise engages all your senses, redirecting focus from internal turmoil to external reality. Sensory grounding is another method where you focus on your senses, such as feeling the texture of an object or listening to the ambient sounds around you. Physical grounding, like feeling your feet on the ground, reminds you of your connection to the earth, encouraging stability and presence. These exercises can be practiced anywhere, making them versatile tools for managing anxiety.

Grounding methods are instrumental during episodes of high anxiety or panic attacks when emotions feel overwhelming. They can also be beneficial before or after triggering events, providing a buffer to help manage emotional responses. For example, if you anticipate a stressful conversation, grounding beforehand can steady your nerves, while grounding afterward can help decompress and process emotions. The beauty of grounding is its adaptability; these techniques can be employed whenever you need to center yourself, offering a reliable way to regain control amidst chaos.

Personalizing grounding techniques to fit your needs can enhance their effectiveness. Consider combining grounding with other practices, like deep breathing, to amplify their calming effects. Another idea would be creating a grounding toolkit filled with objects that help focus the mind. This might include a smooth stone to hold or a calming scent to inhale. Having these readily available tools ensures that you're prepared to ground yourself whenever needed, making grounding an integral part of your emotional regulation repertoire.

Daily Mindfulness Practices

Mindfulness is the practice of being fully present and engaged with the moment. It involves non-judgmental awareness of your thoughts, feelings, and surroundings. For those managing anxious attachment, mindfulness can be incredibly beneficial. It lets you step back from anxious thoughts, offering a clearer perspective. By being present, you reduce stress and improve mental clarity. This approach increases acceptance and compassion toward oneself, which are essential elements in managing anxiety and building self-worth. Practicing mindfulness creates space for calmness and clarity, breaking free from the cycle of anxiousness and rumination.

Incorporating mindfulness into your daily routine can start with simple exercises. Mindful breathing exercises focus on each inhale and exhale, letting thoughts pass without judgment. A body scan meditation guides you through noticing sensations from head to toe, promoting relaxation and awareness. Mindful observation of surroundings encourages noticing details in your environment, like the colors and shapes around you. Mindful eating invites you to savor each bite, paying attention to texture and flavor. These exercises ground you in the moment, providing a refuge from the whirlwind of anxious thoughts that often accompany anxious attachment.

Mindfulness impacts anxious attachment by helping you recognize and manage triggers. It allows you to see patterns in your thoughts and behaviors, reducing their power over you. When you stay present, you minimize rumination and overthinking, two culprits that often exacerbate anxiety. This heightened awareness enhances emotional regulation, giving you tools to navigate relationships with more stability and understanding. Mindfulness also helps you respond, rather than react, to stressors, creating a buffer between your emotions and actions. This approach fosters a sense of control and empowerment, essential for those seeking to overcome anxious attachment.

Incorporating mindfulness into everyday life can be seamless and straightforward. Consider finding mindful moments during daily activities, such as brushing your teeth or walking. These brief pauses can anchor you throughout the day. Dedicate time specifically for mindfulness practice through meditation, deep breathing, or reflection. Embrace mindfulness during household chores or conversations, focusing on each task or dialogue with intention. During my healing process, the best mindfulness trick that helped me was verbalizing what I was doing, which helped me reach my goal out loud and not internally in my head. I would say it aloud, and this made a huge difference. It's as if you are hearing someone else tell your accomplishments to you and not allowing the internal voice to be silenced or criticized. Tracking your mindfulness progress can enhance this practice. Keep a mindfulness journal to reflect on changes in mood and stress levels, and set mindfulness goals to monitor your growth. This ongoing reflection helps reinforce the benefits of mindfulness, ensuring it becomes a lasting part of your routine.

"When we create peace and harmony and balance in our minds, we will find it in our lives."

Louise Hay

Visualization Exercises for Security

"Within you, there is a stillness and a sanctuary to which you can retreat at any time and be yourself."

Hermann Hesse

Think about a time and place where you felt at ease and entered a space where stress and anxiety didn't exist, a sanctuary of calm and safety. This is the power of visualization—a mental practice where you create vivid images to evoke feelings of security and comfort. For those with anxious attachment, visualization can be a vital tool. It helps reduce anxiety by allowing you to mentally transport yourself to a place of peace and control, enhancing emotional well-being. Imagine crafting a mental image of a safe place, a haven where you feel completely at ease. For some, this could be imagining a day at the beach and relaxing in the sun. For others, it may be in the mountains in a cabin. For me, it was imagining coming down a grand staircase, and with each step I took toward my family at the bottom of the stairs, I felt more at ease. This mental sanctuary can serve as a retreat during times of stress, providing a sense of control and tranquility.

To begin with basic visualization exercises, find a quiet place to sit comfortably. Close your eyes and visualize a place where you feel safe. It could be a beach, a forest, or a cozy room. Focus on the details—the colors, the sounds, the scents. Allow yourself to immerse in this environment fully. You can also engage in guided imagery, imagining a loving presence beside you, offering support and reassurance. This presence could be a loved one or an abstract figure symbolizing security. Visualization can also extend to personal goals. Picture yourself achieving a goal and feeling the emotions associated with that success. This not only boosts confidence but also reinforces a positive mindset.

Incorporating visualization into daily routines can be seamless. Consider starting your day with a morning visualization session to set a calm and focused tone. As you wake, take a few minutes to visualize your safe place or a goal you are working toward. Similarly, bedtime is an ideal time for visualization. Allow these images to replace any lingering stress or anxiety, leading to a restful sleep. Pause and visualize your sanctuary during stressful moments, combining this with deep breathing to enhance the calming effect. Integrating visualization into your daily life builds a mental toolkit that supports emotional resilience and security.

Meditation Techniques to Soothe Your Mind

Guided meditation offers a peaceful refuge in your mind, providing the structure and focus needed to calm an anxious heart. For those with anxious attachment, guided meditation is incredibly beneficial. It creates a safe space where the mind can rest, reducing anxiety and stress levels significantly. You cultivate emotional stability and heightened focus by directing your attention to specific areas—such as breath or loving-kindness. This mental clarity enhances self-awareness and helps you navigate emotional storms more easily. When you're anchored in meditation, the chaos of anxious thoughts fades, leaving room for calmness and insight.

You can explore various guided meditation scripts, each tailored to specific needs. Loving-kindness meditation fosters self-compassion, encouraging you to extend warmth to yourself and others. Protective visualization meditation allows you to imagine a shield around you, offering comfort and security. On the other hand, focused attention meditation trains your mind to concentrate on a single point, such as your breath or a mantra, enhancing mental discipline. Grounding meditation helps you stay present by connecting you to the here and now, reducing feeling overwhelmed. Body scan meditation guides you in observing sensations from head to toe, promoting relaxation and awareness.

Breath awareness meditation invites you to focus on each inhale and exhale, centering your mind and body.

Meditation may seem daunting for beginners, but a few practical tips can make the process smoother. Start with short sessions, perhaps five to ten minutes, gradually increasing as you grow more comfortable. Find a quiet and comfortable space where you won't be disturbed, allowing yourself to engage with the practice entirely. Consider using meditation apps or recordings, which provide guidance and structure, making it easier to follow along. These tools benefit those new to meditation, offering support and encouragement as you build your practice.

Integrating meditation into daily life can transform these moments of calm into a consistent practice. Set a regular meditation schedule that fits your lifestyle, ensuring you dedicate time to this restorative activity. Combine meditation with other relaxation techniques, such as deep breathing or visualization, to enhance its effects. Reflecting on your meditation experiences in a journal can provide insights into your progress and the impact on your emotional well-being. This reflection reinforces the benefits of meditation, encouraging you to maintain the practice even amidst life's challenges.

Cognitive-Behavioral Strategies for Managing Anxiety

Cognitive-behavioral therapy, or CBT, is a well-regarded approach in psychology that focuses on the interplay between thoughts, feelings, and behaviors. It is based on the principle that our thoughts influence our emotions and behavior. By identifying and transforming negative thought patterns, CBT aims to alleviate emotional distress and encourage healthier behaviors. This approach is particularly beneficial for managing anxiety, as it provides structured techniques to understand and change the thought processes that often fuel anxious feelings. One of the core elements of CBT is cognitive restructuring, which involves challenging and reframing negative thoughts. This can transform how you perceive situations, reducing anxiety and having a more positive mindset.

Behavioral activation is another key strategy in CBT, emphasizing engagement in positive activities to boost mood and counteract depressive tendencies. You can create a buffer against anxiety by intentionally scheduling enjoyable activities, increasing overall well-being. Exposure therapy, a gradual approach to confronting fears, helps desensitize anxiety responses. By facing feared situations in a controlled manner, you build resilience and diminish the power these fears hold over you. These techniques, while seemingly simple, require practice and commitment but can lead to profound changes in how you experience and respond to anxiety.

To implement CBT techniques, consider starting with thought records. This involves logging negative thoughts as they arise and analyzing them to identify cognitive distortions. Over time, you'll learn to reframe these thoughts, reducing their impact. Activity scheduling, another practical exercise, involves planning activities that bring joy and fulfillment, breaking the cycle of inactivity that anxiety often perpetuates. Gradual exposure plans can be crafted to systematically confront fears, starting with less intimidating scenarios and gradually progressing to more challenging ones. These exercises not only help manage anxiety but also empower you to take control of your emotional responses.

Real-life examples illustrate the transformative power of CBT. Take Lisa, who struggled with fear of abandonment. She learned to challenge her assumptions by using cognitive restructuring, replacing them with more balanced perspectives. This shift allowed her to build more secure relationships. Similarly, Michael faced relationship anxiety, feeling overwhelmed by his partner's social interactions. Through behavioral activation, he rediscovered hobbies and social activities that boosted his mood, enhancing his relationship satisfaction. These stories highlight how practical CBT strategies can be, offering hope and concrete steps for those seeking to manage anxiety effectively.

Interactive Element: Emotion Regulation Journal Prompt

Reflect on a recent situation where your emotions felt overwhelming. Write down what triggered the emotion, how you responded, and any accompanying thoughts. Then, explore how you might apply emotional regulation techniques, such as deep breathing or cognitive restructuring, in similar situations in the future. This exercise can be done more than once, providing valuable insights into your emotional patterns and helping you develop healthier responses.

We are shaped by our thoughts; we become what we think. When the mind is pure, joy follows like a shadow that never leaves."

Buddha

THE MIND IS A POWERFUL TOOL

CHAPTER FIVE

Holistic Healing Approaches

"Our bodies communicate to us clearly and specifically, if we are willing to listen."

Shakti Gawain

The Role of Nutrition in Emotional Health

F eeling a fog lift from your mind, not because of a sudden epiphany but due to a simple change in what you eat, can feel amazing. Every bite you take fuels your body and brain, influencing how you think, feel, and respond to stress. The link between diet and mental health is intricate and transformative, highlighting the power food has in shaping our emotional landscape. Nutritional psychiatry, a burgeoning field, delves into this connection, revealing how our dietary choices can either support mental well-being or contribute to emotional turmoil.

Nutrient-rich foods are like premium fuel for your brain, bolstering its function and structure. Consuming high-quality foods filled with vitamins, minerals, and antioxidants can protect your brain from oxidative stress, an imbalance in the body that damages cells and is linked to mood disorders. For instance, a diet abundant in omega-3 fatty acids—found in fish and flaxseeds—has been correlated with lower rates of depression. These nutrients are crucial to brain health, supporting cognitive function and emotional stability. Vitamins like B6, B12, and folic acid are equally important, influencing mood regulation and reducing symptoms of anxiety and depression. They assist in producing neurotransmitters, the brain's chemical messengers that impact mood and emotions. Maintaining a balanced intake of proteins, fats, and carbohydrates also ensures that your body receives a steady supply of energy and nutrients, supporting physical and emotional health.

On the other hand, diets high in sugar and processed foods can have a detrimental effect on your mental health. High sugar intake can exacerbate mood disorders by promoting inflammation and oxidative stress, which negatively impacts brain function. Processed foods often contain artificial additives and preservatives that can affect gut health, further influencing mood and behavior. The gut-brain axis, a communication network between the gut and the brain, highlights how gut bacteria can impact mental health. A healthy gut environment, supported by a fiber-rich diet and fermented foods, can enhance mood and energy levels.

In contrast, poor dietary choices can disrupt gut health, leading to increased anxiety and depression.

Hydration is another crucial component of mental well-being that is often overlooked. Adequate water intake is essential for maintaining bodily functions, including those of the brain. Dehydration can lead to fatigue, difficulty concentrating, and mood swings, all of which can aggravate feelings of anxiety and depression. Drinking sufficient water throughout the day is vital to support mental health and ensure your body and mind remain well-hydrated. Reducing the intake of dehydrating substances like caffeine and alcohol is also beneficial, as they can disrupt sleep patterns, further impacting mental health.

Focusing on a nutrient-rich diet and maintaining proper hydration can create a supportive environment for your mental well-being. These changes may seem small, but their impact can be significant in balancing and enhancing your emotional and physical health.

Interactive Element: Reflective Journaling Prompt

Consider your current diet and how it makes you feel emotionally. The easiest way to accomplish this is to write it down in a food journal and document what you eat and how it makes you feel during or afterward. Some may find it beneficial to do a photo journal, take a photo of what you are eating, and note how you feel. Do patterns or foods seem to affect your mood positively or negatively? Take a few minutes each day to jot down your observations. Reflect on how you might introduce more nutrient-rich foods into your meals. This simple practice can help you become more mindful of the connection between your diet and mental health, guiding you toward choices that support emotional well-being.

Physical Activity and Emotional Well-Being

Taking a brisk walk and feeling the air fill your lungs allows your worries to dissipate as you take in each breath. Physical activity offers more than just fitness; it profoundly impacts emotional well-being. Regular exercise reduces symptoms of anxiety and depression, acting as a natural antidote to stress. When you exercise, your body releases endorphins, those feel-good chemicals that can elevate your mood and create a euphoria. These natural mood boosters help counteract the effects of stress hormones like cortisol, which can wreak havoc on your body and mind when left unchecked. Moreover, exercise enhances sleep quality, a crucial component of emotional health. Better sleep means more energy, improved mood, and greater resilience in facing life's challenges.

Different types of physical activities offer unique benefits for emotional health. Aerobic exercises, such as running, cycling, and swimming, are particularly effective at reducing anxiety and depression. They get your heart pumping and your mood soaring. With its focus on breath and movement, yoga provides a calming effect on the mind and body, allowing for inner peace and balance. Strength training builds confidence and resilience, empowering you to face physical and emotional challenges. Even a simple walk in nature, known as forest bathing, can profoundly affect your mood. The tranquility of natural surroundings soothes the mind, allowing stress to melt away.

Combining physical activity with mindfulness enhances these benefits, creating a practice known as mindful movement. Mindful yoga and tai chi focus on the connection between breath and movement, promoting a deep sense of awareness and presence. Engaging in mindful walking or running encourages you to pay attention to the sensations in your body, the rhythm of your breath, and the world around you. This practice enhances the physical benefits of exercise and cultivates mental clarity and emotional balance.

Developing a sustainable exercise routine is key to maintaining these benefits over time. Start by setting realistic and achievable goals that fit your lifestyle. Identify activities you genuinely enjoy, as this will make it easier to stick to your routine. Whether it's a morning jog, an evening yoga session, or a weekend hike, incorporating exercise into your daily routine can become a rewarding habit. The key is consistency, allowing you to reap physical activity's mental and emotional rewards.

Sleep Hygiene for Better Mental Health

Waking up from a night full of deep, uninterrupted sleep feeling refreshed and ready to face the day isn't just a luxury; it's a vital part of maintaining emotional well-being. Quality sleep allows your brain to process emotions, sort through memories, and reset for the challenges ahead. During these hours of rest, your brain works through the intricate web of feelings and experiences, helping you wake up with a clearer mind and a more balanced mood. When sleep is disrupted, the consequences are noticeable. Lack of sleep can heighten anxiety, impair your mood, and diminish cognitive function, making it harder to navigate daily stressors. Emotional regulation suffers, and simple tasks can feel overwhelmingly difficult.

Consider transforming your bedroom into a tranquil retreat to create an environment conducive to restorative sleep. A cool, dark, and quiet room can dramatically improve sleep quality. The right mattress and pillows, tailored to your comfort preferences, are investments in your well-being. Removing electronic devices from your bedroom can eliminate the blue light that disrupts your natural sleep cycle. By creating a space dedicated solely to rest, you signal to your body and mind that it's time to wind down, easing the transition from wakefulness to sleep. If removing or creating these conditions is not possible, get creative. If you can not remove the electronic devices, then make sure they are turned off and out of view as you lay down for sleep. If you can't afford the newer mattress or pillow that may feel better, try flipping the mattress around and laying on a different side; this will allow your body to find a more comfortable spot.

Establishing healthy sleep habits can further enhance your nightly rest. Consistency is key; try to go to bed and wake up at the same time every day, even on weekends. This routine helps regulate your body's internal clock, making falling and staying asleep easier. Developing a relaxing bedtime routine signals your body that it's time to unwind. Consider reading a book, taking a warm bath, or practicing gentle stretches. It's also wise to avoid caffeine and heavy meals before bedtime, as these can interfere with your ability to drift off peacefully.

Several techniques can help improve sleep quality. Mindfulness and relaxation exercises before bed can quiet the mind and prepare you for rest. Progressive muscle relaxation (PMR), which involves tensing and relaxing each muscle group, can reduce physical tension and promote relaxation. This is a method I use quite often. I will set up a guided PMR that I listen to right as I'm lying down to sleep. I put it on my phone, which will be the last thing I do before putting it away and not looking at it for the rest of the evening. Keeping a sleep journal or using a smartwatch to track sleep patterns can provide insights into your habits, helping you identify areas for improvement. These strategies, tailored to your preferences and lifestyle, pave the way for more restful nights and brighter days.

Exploring Creative Outlets for Emotional Expression

A blank canvas stands before you. As you begin to paint, the swirl of colors captures your emotions, giving form to feelings that words sometimes fail to express. Engaging in creative activities like art, music, or writing provides more than just a pastime; it becomes a powerful means to channel emotions and enhance your emotional well-being. Whether it's the gentle stroke of a brush, the rhythmic movement of dance, or the flow of words on a page, these creative outlets allow you to process and express emotions in ways that can alleviate stress and anxiety. By immersing yourself in creative pursuits, you cultivate a deeper self-awareness, gaining insights into your inner world, and find not only a promising way of helping emotional regulation but an entertaining one as well.

Many forms of creative expression can benefit your mental health. Art and drawing offer a visual language for your emotions, allowing you to explore and resolve inner conflicts. The soothing melodies of music can transport you, evoking memories and feelings, while dance provides a physical release, letting your body express what your heart feels. Creative writing and journaling serve as a reflective practice where you can articulate your thoughts and experiences, gaining clarity and perspective. Crafting and DIY projects engage your hands and mind, promoting a sense of achievement and focus. Consider using a punching bag as a stress reliever, as I do. The most extensive advice for this one is to let out what emotion is weighing on you with each punch. As I punch the bag, I will say the word, feeling, or instance that caused the emotional build-up aloud. These activities offer an escape and help you better understand yourself, enhancing your ability to navigate life's challenges with grace and creativity.

Incorporating creativity into your routine doesn't have to be daunting. Start by setting aside dedicated time for creative pursuits, a few minutes each day, or a more extended weekend session. This commitment to creativity becomes a gift you give yourself, a space where you can explore and experiment without judgment. Consider joining a creative community or class to connect with like-minded individuals, sharing inspiration and support. These connections can enrich your creative experiences, providing new perspectives and encouragement. Combining creativity with relaxation practices, such as meditative drawing or mindful music listening, further enhances the benefits, creating a holistic approach to emotional well-being.

Interactive Element: Creative Exploration Exercise

Choose a creative activity that resonates with you, whether painting, writing, or another form of expression. Set a timer for 15 minutes and immerse yourself in the process, focusing on the sensations and emotions that arise. Let go of any expectations of perfection and enjoy the act of creating. Afterward, take a moment to reflect on how the experience made you feel. Did it bring clarity, relief, or joy? Record your thoughts in a journal to track your creative journey and its impact on your emotional health. This simple exercise can open doors to new insights and healing, nurturing your mind and spirit.

Emotional Freedom Techniques (EFT) for Anxiety

Emotional Freedom Techniques (EFT) roots are at the crossroads of ancient wisdom and modern psychology. Developed in the late 20th century, EFT combines the principles of acupuncture with psychological strategies to alleviate anxiety. Instead of needles, it uses tapping on specific meridian points while focusing on negative emotions, creating a unique blend of cognitive and physical techniques. By tapping on these points—often around the face and upper body—you can release energy blockages that contribute to emotional distress. This practice, sometimes called "tapping," allows you to address both the mind and body simultaneously, providing a holistic approach to managing anxiety.

The benefits of EFT for emotional healing are profound. By engaging in this practice, you can release negative emotions and limiting beliefs that have long held you captive. Tapping while acknowledging your feelings helps reduce stress's physical and emotional symptoms, providing relief and clarity. As you tap, the tension in your body eases, and your mind becomes more receptive to positive change. This process can lead to a significant reduction in anxiety and emotional distress, offering a path toward greater emotional freedom and resilience.

To begin with EFT, identify the issue or emotion you wish to address. It could be anxiety about a specific event, a recurring fear, or a sense of insecurity. Once you pinpoint the emotion, create a setup statement acknowledging your feelings while offering acceptance. For example, "Even though I feel anxious, I deeply and completely accept myself." This statement is a foundation for tapping, grounding you in self-compassion. Next, proceed with tapping on the meridian points in sequence: the side of the hand, the top of the head, the eyebrow, the side of the eye, under the eye, under the nose, the chin, the collarbone, and under the arm. As you tap each point, repeat a reminder phrase that encapsulates your emotion, allowing you to stay focused and present throughout the exercise.

When addressing the fear of abandonment, your script might begin with, "Even though I fear being left alone, I choose to feel secure." For relationship anxiety, consider a statement like, "Even though I worry about our future, I accept where we are now." If self-doubt and insecurity plague you, you might use, "Even though I question my worth, I am learning to value myself." These scripts provide a starting point, but feel free to adapt them to suit your personal experiences and emotions. The key is to remain honest and compassionate with yourself as you tap, creating a safe space for healing and growth.

Consider Lisa, who struggled with anxiety during conflicts with her partner. By incorporating EFT into her routine, she found a way to navigate these interactions more calmly and clearly. The tapping process allowed her to release built-up tension, making it easier to communicate her needs and listen empathetically. Similarly, David faced chronic stress that seemed impossible. Regular EFT practice became his refuge, offering relief and a sense of control over his emotional state. Through tapping, David was able to confront his stressors with newfound resilience, transforming his relationship with anxiety. These stories illustrate the potential of EFT to create meaningful change, offering hope and empowerment to those seeking emotional healing.

Chapter Six

Finding Comfort Within

"A moment of self-compassion can change your entire day. A string of such moments can change the course of your life."

Chris Germer

The Reassurance Journal

I magine coming home after a long day, your mind swirling with worries and doubts. You sit quietly, allowing the silence to envelop you, and open a journal that feels like an old friend. With a pen in hand, you begin to write about your day, thoughts, and emotions. This simple act of journaling becomes a sanctuary, a place to explore your inner world without fear of judgment.

Keeping a reassurance journal is a practice that offers profound benefits for emotional well-being. It's a space for self-reassurance, where you can record positive affirmations and comforting thoughts, building a reservoir of internal strength and security.

A reassurance journal serves as a personal haven, providing solace in times of uncertainty. By recording affirmations and reflections, you reduce reliance on external validation, learning to trust your voice and instincts. This practice enables internal sources of comfort, reinforcing your ability to self-soothe and find peace within as you document your thoughts; a sense of positivity and self-awareness blossoms, illuminating the strengths and successes that may have been overlooked. The journal becomes a mirror reflecting your growth, resilience, and potential, a tool that nurtures self-compassion and empowerment. The simplicity of seeing the accomplishments written on the page is more powerful than trying to think about all of them in your head.

Starting a reassurance journal is a simple yet transformative process. Begin by choosing a journal that resonates with you- a beautifully bound notebook or a digital app. Set aside time each day to write, creating a routine that signals a pause from the chaos of daily life. This dedicated time becomes an opportunity to focus on your needs and emotions, deepening your connection with yourself. As you write, incorporate positive affirmations and comforting statements. These words of encouragement remind you of your strength and capabilities, countering self-doubt and anxiety. Reflect on past successes and strengths, acknowledging the achievements that have shaped your journey. This reflection reinforces a sense of accomplishment and self-worth, bolstering your confidence in navigating future challenges. Keep in mind this journal is to empower you and boost your self-worth. Write positively and with kindness to yourself.

Sample entries and prompts can guide your journaling practice, providing a framework for exploration and reflection. Beginning with a prompt like, "Today, I reminded myself that I am capable and strong because..." encourages you to focus on your resilience and abilities to feel empowered. Another prompt might be, "A positive affirmation I will focus on today is..." By selecting an affirmation, you create an intention for the day, a mantra that supports your emotional well-being. Reflecting on moments of security and peace can also be insightful. Write about a time when you felt secure and at ease, exploring the factors contributing to this comfort. This reflection helps identify the conditions that feel emotionally safe, which will guide you in implementing them more intentionally in your life.

Visual Element: Example Reassurance Journal Entry

Date: March 4th

Today, I reminded myself I am capable and strong because I handled a challenging meeting confidently and clearly. Today, I will focus on a positive affirmation: "I am worthy of love and respect." I felt secure and at peace when I spent time in the garden, surrounded by the calming presence of nature.

Through the practice of reassurance journaling, you embark on a path of self-discovery and healing. This simple yet powerful tool offers a space to explore your thoughts, affirm your strengths, and nurture a sense of inner peace. As you continue to write, you build a foundation of self-awareness and resilience, finding comfort and security within yourself.

Incorporating Gratitude Practices

Imagine waking up and starting your day with a simple thought: "What am I grateful for today?" Gratitude is more than just a fleeting feeling; it's a powerful psychological tool that shifts your focus to the positive aspects of life. You create a mindset that enhances overall well-being and happiness by emphasizing what you appreciate. Gratitude profoundly affects brain chemistry, promoting the release of dopamine and serotonin, neurotransmitters linked to pleasure and mood stabilization. This biochemical shift reduces stress and anxiety, providing a buffer against the challenges of daily life. Moreover, gratitude nurtures stronger social connections, as expressing appreciation to others builds trust and deepens bonds.

Cultivating gratitude can be achieved through practical exercises that fit seamlessly into your daily routine. Consider keeping a gratitude journal, where you jot down a few things you're thankful for each day. This practice reinforces positive thinking and provides a tangible record of moments of joy and contentment. This can go along with your reassurance journal. Writing gratitude letters to loved ones is another powerful exercise. These letters offer a heartfelt way to express appreciation, strengthen relationships, and promote a supportive environment. Daily gratitude reflections, where you pause to consider what you're grateful for, can transform mundane moments into opportunities for joy. This practice is excellent to pair with positive everyday affirmations. Make them gratitude affirmations, and you've hit two nails with one hammer.

The impact of gratitude on relationships is profound. Expressing appreciation to partners and friends creates a positive feedback loop that enhances relationship dynamics. This expression of gratitude builds a foundation of mutual respect and empathy, encouraging a supportive and understanding environment. Over time, relationships prioritizing gratitude become more resilient, weathering challenges with greater ease and grace.

The most significant impact on my relationship with my husband was ensuring we gave each other gratitude. You always think, "They know I'm grateful for this," but saying it aloud to them proves to be more powerful and impactful. My husband and I have made it our routine to show gratitude towards one another whenever possible. This has made a stronger relationship and less "Is he grateful?" thoughts in my head.

Incorporating gratitude into daily life doesn't require grand gestures; it's about making small, consistent efforts. Begin or end your day with a gratitude ritual, taking a moment to reflect on the positives. Share your gratitude with family and friends to create a culture of appreciation in your social circles. Consider using gratitude prompts or apps to guide your reflections. Prompts like "What made me smile today?" or "Who am I thankful for in my life?" can inspire deeper introspection and recognition of the good in your life.

Embracing gratitude opens the door to a more fulfilling and connected existence. As you integrate these practices into your life, you'll likely notice a shift in your perspective, leading to greater emotional resilience and satisfaction. Gratitude transforms your outlook and enriches your relationships, creating a ripple effect of positivity that extends beyond yourself.

Daily Routines for Emotional Stability

The feeling of waking up each day with a clear sense of purpose and direction is the power of a well-structured routine. Having a daily routine can do wonders for your emotional health. It provides the structure and predictability that many of us crave, offering a safe haven from the chaos and unpredictability of life. Stress and anxiety naturally decrease when you know what to expect each day. You no longer have to expend energy on decision-making for mundane tasks, freeing up mental space for more important things. Regular habits anchor your day, grounding you and enhancing your overall mental well-being. The predictability of a routine brings comfort, reducing the mental load of decision fatigue and allowing you to focus on what truly matters. This sense of order is particularly beneficial for managing anxious attachment, as it creates a stable foundation upon which to build emotional resilience.

Creating a balanced daily routine involves thoughtful consideration and intentional planning. Start by incorporating mindfulness and relaxation practices into your day. These moments of calm can act as touchstones, reminding you to pause and breathe amidst the business. Balance is key, so ensure that your routine includes work, leisure, and self-care activities. Scheduling regular physical activity is also crucial, as movement benefits the body and invigorates the mind, helping to dispel anxiety and stress. By weaving these elements into your daily life, you create a tapestry of activities that nurture both body and soul.

Consider a morning routine that begins with meditation, journaling, and a healthy breakfast. This sets a positive tone for the day, grounding you in mindfulness and reflection before stepping into the world. As midday approaches, take mindful breaks. Practice deep breathing exercises to refresh and refocus your mind. These short pauses can profoundly impact you, allowing you to return to your tasks with renewed clarity and energy. In the evening, engage in relaxation techniques such as gentle stretches or a warm bath. Conclude your day with gratitude journaling, reflecting on the positive moments and experiences. This practice will give you a sense of appreciation and encourage a peaceful transition to rest, nurturing emotional well-being.

Routines should not feel rigid or constraining. Personalizing and adapting them to fit your lifestyle is important, ensuring they remain effective and enjoyable. Flexibility is key. Allow yourself the freedom to add or remove activities based on their impact on your well-being. Regularly review your routine, assessing what's working and what needs adjustment. This ongoing evaluation ensures that your routine evolves with you, remaining relevant and supportive as your needs change. Embrace the idea that routines are living entities capable of growing and transforming alongside you. By maintaining this adaptability, you cultivate a routine that genuinely supports your emotional health, providing stability and comfort in life's ever-changing landscape.

Coping Mechanisms for Relationship Anxiety

You're in a relationship, yet a shadow of doubt often lingers. You question if your partner truly cares or if they might leave at any moment. This fear of abandonment is a common anxiety in relationships, rooted in past experiences where love felt uncertain. It can manifest as insecurity about your partner's feelings, leading you to overanalyze their words and actions. You might find yourself replaying conversations in your head, searching for hidden meanings, or worrying about things that haven't even happened. This overthinking can spiral into a cycle of rumination, leaving you emotionally exhausted and disconnected from the present moment.

To manage these anxieties, adopting healthy coping mechanisms is crucial. Open communication with your partner is foundational. Sharing your feelings and concerns can lead to understanding and trust, creating a safe space where both of you feel heard. Setting and respecting boundaries is important and ensuring both partners feel comfortable and secure. This might mean agreeing on how often to communicate during busy days or setting aside time for meaningful conversations. Practicing mindfulness and presence during interactions can also help. Focusing on the present moment reduces the noise of anxious thoughts, allowing you to truly connect with your partner.

Engaging in specific exercises can further support these strategies. Reflective journaling is a powerful tool for processing relationship anxieties. You gain clarity and insight into your emotional patterns by writing about your fears and responses. This practice helps you understand triggers and develop healthier ways to cope. Guided imagery is another technique that can be beneficial. Close your eyes and visualize positive relationship outcomes, imagining a scenario where both you and your partner feel secure and content. This mental exercise can shift your focus from potential problems to possibilities, giving a more optimistic outlook. Grounding techniques can be invaluable before and after difficult conversations. Whether taking a few deep breaths or focusing on the sensations in your body, grounding helps anchor you, reducing the intensity of emotional reactions.

Consider Anna, who struggled with relationship anxiety. She realized that her fears often stemmed from assumptions rather than reality. By practicing open communication, she learned to voice her concerns without blame, inviting her partner into a dialogue of mutual understanding. This openness strengthened their bond, reducing her anxiety and increasing trust. Then there's Mark, who found solace in mindfulness. He noticed that his anxious thoughts often revolved around imagined scenarios. By staying present in his interactions, he could connect more authentically with his partner, easing his fears and enhancing their relationship. These examples illustrate that with intention and effort, it is possible to navigate relationship anxiety by building resilient and nurturing connections.

Creating a Personal Self-Care Plan

A self-care plan offers a personalized collection of activities and practices designed to support your overall well-being and is filled with tools that nurture your mind, body, and soul. Self-care is about more than just pampering yourself; it's a vital practice that promotes your physical, mental, and emotional health. Regular self-care helps manage anxiety and build resilience, equipping you with the strength to navigate life's challenges. By prioritizing self-care, you create a foundation of stability and peace, allowing you to approach each day with greater confidence and clarity.

To create a personalized self-care plan, assess your needs and preferences. Consider what aspects of your life require attention and care. Are there areas where you feel drained or overwhelmed? Identifying these needs will guide you in selecting activities that resonate with you. Once you've pinpointed your needs, explore various self-care activities that align with them. Physical activities like exercise, yoga, or walking in nature can invigorate your body and lift your spirits. Relaxation practices like meditation, deep breathing, or aromatherapy offer moments of tranquility and reflection. Creative outlets, like painting, writing, or playing music, provide a space for expression and exploration. Social activities, whether spending time with loved ones or joining a support group, will nurture connection and belonging. By choosing activities that resonate with your unique personality and preferences, you ensure that your self-care plan is both enjoyable and effective.

Scheduling regular self-care practices is essential for embedding them into your routine. As you would set aside time for appointments or commitments, dedicate time each week to engage in self-care activities. This commitment signals to yourself that your well-being is a priority, reinforcing the importance of nurturing yourself. As you integrate these practices into your daily life, you'll likely notice a positive shift in your mood and energy levels as self-care becomes a source of renewal and strength.

Maintaining and adjusting your self-care plan is crucial to keeping it relevant and effective. Regularly review your plan, assessing which activities continue to serve you and which may need modification. Listen to your body and mind's signals, adapting your strategy to meet changing needs and circumstances. Flexibility is key; allow yourself the freedom to explore new activities or let go of those that no longer resonate. By remaining open to change, you cultivate a self-care plan that evolves with you, providing ongoing support and nourishment.

In crafting your self-care plan, remember that it's a living entity—a reflection of your journey toward greater self-awareness and well-being. Treating your self-care plan as a dynamic and responsive tool empowers you to thrive in all aspects of life. This chapter has explored how to create a self-care plan that supports emotional health and resilience, setting the stage for deeper exploration of healing and growth.

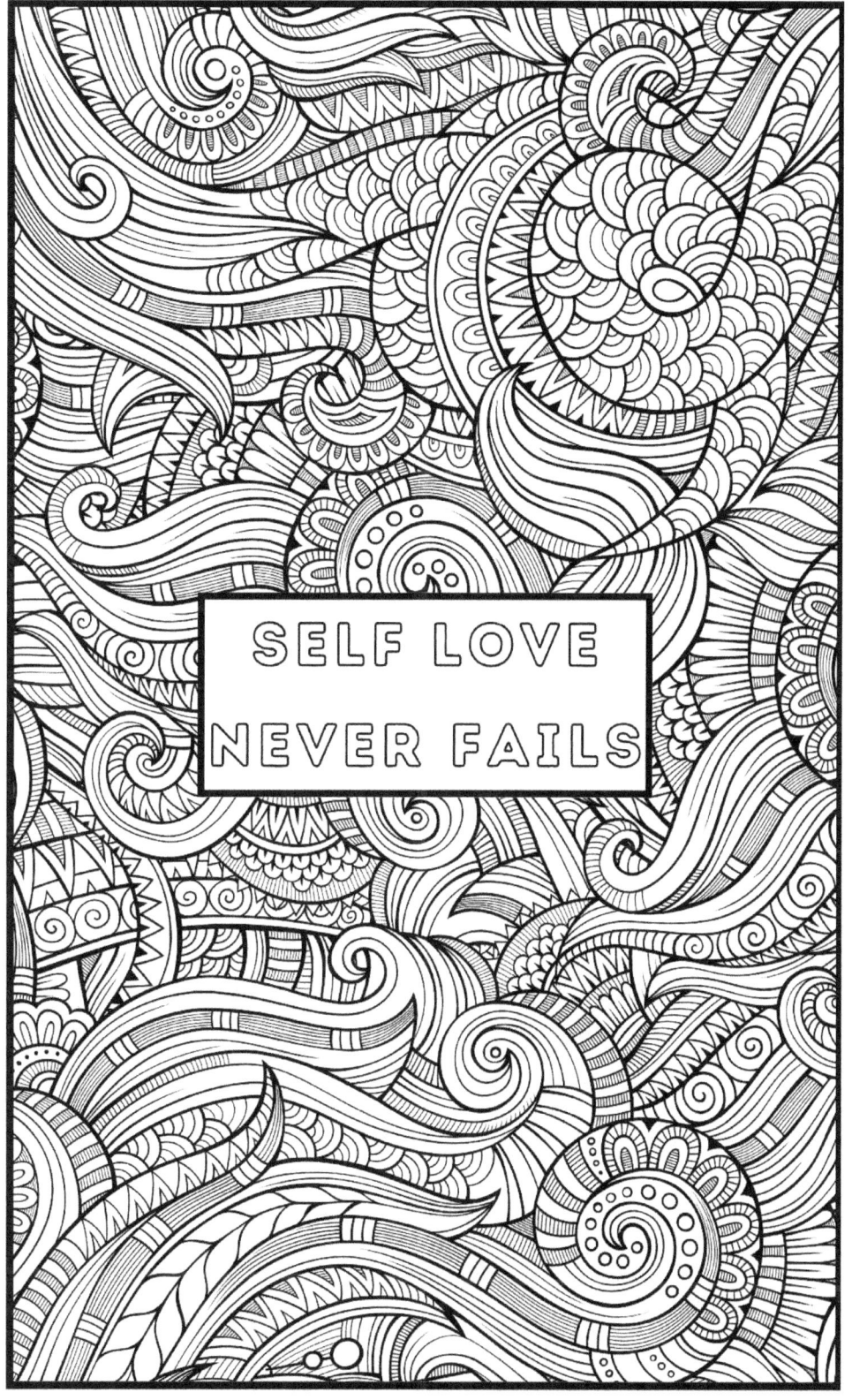

Make a Difference with Your Review: Unlock the Power of Generosity

"The best way to find yourself is to lose yourself in the service of others." – Mahatma Gandhi

Would you help someone like you who is worried and scared about being close to others? My mission is to make understanding anxious attachments easy and less overwhelming for everyone. But to reach more people, I need your help. Most people choose books based on reviews. So, I'm asking you to help a fellow person who is curious about anxious attachment but unsure where to start by leaving a review. It costs nothing and takes less than a minute but could change someone's anxious attachment journey. Your review could help...

...one more person feel less alone and more understood.
...one more person learn how to manage their emotions in a healthy way.
...one more person build stronger, more secure relationships.

To make a difference, simply click the link below or scan the QR code and leave a review:

https://www.amazon.com/review/review-your-purchases/?asin=1966973012

Thank you from the bottom of my heart!
Angelina Peck

CHAPTER SEVEN

Healing Past Wounds

Understanding Inner-Child Work

I magine standing at the edge of a forest, where each tree represents a memory from your past. Some are tall and strong, while others are twisted and gnarled, casting long shadows. These shadows can follow you into adulthood, shaping how you interact with the world and those around you. Understanding and healing these past wounds is crucial to moving forward. An insightful quote to consider: "The past is a place of reference, not a place of residence; the past is a place of learning, not a place of living." This chapter delves into the transformative power of inner-child work, a method that helps you reconcile with your past and nurture the parts of yourself that were neglected or hurt.

Inner-child work is a therapeutic process that involves acknowledging and healing the wounded child within you. This inner child represents your early experiences, emotions, and memories, many of which may have been buried or ignored. By connecting with this part of yourself, you can begin to understand how these early experiences influence your current behaviors and emotional responses. This process involves revisiting the past, not to dwell on it, but to gain insights that can lead to healing and growth. It allows you to address unresolved emotions and unmet needs, stimulating a sense of wholeness and self-compassion.

Engaging in inner-child work requires courage and patience, as it often involves facing painful memories and emotions. However, this exploration can lead to profound healing. By recognizing the unmet needs of your inner child, you can begin to provide the love and care that were absent during your formative years. This can involve activities encouraging self-expression and creativity, allowing your inner child to feel seen and heard. As you nurture this aspect of yourself, you cultivate a sense of safety and security, which can positively impact your self-esteem and relationships. The goal is to integrate the inner child into your adult self, creating a harmonious relationship between past and present.

The journey of inner-child work is unique to each individual, as it involves personal reflection and self-discovery. You may benefit from writing letters to your inner child, offering reassurance and understanding. Visualization exercises can also be powerful, where you imagine meeting your inner child and providing comfort and support. Through these practices, you can gradually heal old wounds and replace negative self-beliefs with compassion and acceptance. This process allows you to let go of past grievances and empowers you to build a new narrative for your life filled with hope, resilience, and self-love.

Interactive Element: Inner-Child Visualization Exercise

Find a quiet space where you can relax without distractions. Close your eyes and take a few deep breaths. Visualize yourself as a child standing in front of you. Notice their expression and body language. What do they need from you? Spend a few moments offering them love, understanding, and reassurance. Imagine embracing them, letting them know they are safe and valued. This exercise can help bridge the gap between past and present, nurturing a deeper connection with your inner child.

Healing Childhood Wounds

Childhood wounds often stem from experiences where our basic emotional needs are unmet. Imagine a child reaching out for affection only to encounter coldness or indifference. This neglect leaves a mark that can persist into adulthood. Emotional unavailability is another culprit, where caregivers might be physically present but emotionally distant, leaving the child feeling invisible and unheard. Inconsistent caregiving adds to the complexity, where a caregiver is nurturing one day and they are detached or preoccupied the next. This unpredictability sends mixed signals, confusing the child and hindering their emotional development. Over time, these experiences shape how we see ourselves and interact with others.

These early wounds often manifest as persistent feelings of inadequacy and insecurity as adults. You might find yourself questioning your worth, always seeking reassurance and validation. This constant doubt makes trusting others difficult. Forming secure attachments becomes challenging, as past experiences have taught you that love can be fleeting and conditional. The shadow of these childhood wounds looms large, affecting your self-perception and relationships. You might build walls to protect yourself, keeping others at arm's length to avoid the pain of potential rejection. Yet, this protective mechanism often leads to isolation and loneliness, reinforcing the very fears you seek to escape.

It is crucial to reflect on past experiences and identify the specific moments that left a mark to begin healing from these childhood wounds. This requires honesty and courage as you face memories that might be painful or long buried. Journaling can be a helpful tool in this process, allowing you to explore your past safely and structured. Writing down your thoughts and memories can bring clarity and understanding, helping you see patterns that influence your current behavior. Acknowledging these wounds is the first step toward healing, as it allows you to confront the emotions and beliefs that have held you back.

Seeking professional therapy can provide deeper healing and support. A therapist can guide you through the complexities of your past, offering insights and strategies to address unresolved emotions. Therapy creates a safe space to explore your feelings and develop healthier coping mechanisms. It allows you to process the anger, sadness, and fear that childhood wounds often generate. Through therapeutic techniques like grounding, recalling, and sharing, you can begin to release the hold these wounds have on your life. This healing process, though sometimes uncomfortable, is ultimately rewarding. It frees the energy spent on past trauma, allowing you to embrace new, positive experiences and build a life filled with love and connection.

"Scars show us where we have been, they don't dictate where we are going."

David Rossi

Nurturing Your Inner Child

Full of wonder and curiosity, a young child reaches out for love and validation. Now, imagine that this child is a part of you, always present, carrying the echoes of your past. Nurturing your inner child is crucial for ongoing emotional health because it provides the love and care that may have been missing in your childhood. It's about building a sense of safety and security within yourself, creating an environment where your inner child feels valued and understood. Doing so creates a foundation of self-acceptance and resilience that supports your emotional well-being.

To nurture your inner child, engage in playful and creative activities that bring joy and fulfillment. This could be as simple as revisiting a childhood hobby, like painting or building with blocks. These activities allow your inner child to express itself freely, reconnecting with the joy and imagination of youth. Additionally, practicing self-soothing techniques is essential to comfort your inner child during times of stress or anxiety. This might involve wrapping yourself in a cozy blanket, sipping a warm drink, or listening to calming music. These small acts of kindness reassure your inner child that it is safe and cherished.

Daily self-nurturing affirmations can reinforce this nurturing process. Start your day with affirmations for self-love and acceptance, such as "I am worthy of love and kindness" or "I deserve happiness and peace." These affirmations can help shift your mindset, replacing self-doubt with confidence and compassion. Creating a self-care routine that includes activities your inner child enjoys is another powerful way to nurture this part of yourself. Schedule regular time for activities that bring you joy, whether it's dancing in your living room or playing a musical instrument. This routine nurtures your inner child and strengthens your overall emotional health.

Consider the story of Rachel, who rediscovered joy through creative play. She loved to draw as a child, but she abandoned this passion as life became more demanding. By setting aside time each week to sketch and paint, Rachel found a renewed sense of happiness and fulfillment. Her inner child felt seen and heard, and this creative expression became vital to her self-care routine. Similarly, James struggled with feeling insecure and anxious. He began using self-soothing techniques, like practicing deep breathing and visualization exercises, to calm his inner child. Over time, these practices helped him feel more secure and grounded, enhancing his emotional resilience and well-being.

Forgiving Yourself and Others

"To have faith is to trust yourself to the water. When you swim you don't grab hold of the water, because if you do you will sink and drown. Instead, you relax and float."

Alan Watts

Forgiveness is often described as an act of liberation, freeing oneself from the weight of past grievances that can tether one to pain and regret. In healing, forgiveness is crucial because it allows us to release the emotional burdens we've carried, creating space for peace and closure. Imagine holding a grudge as if it were a heavy stone. You carry this stone daily, which uses all your energy, leaving you drained and weary. By choosing to forgive, you set down this weight, allowing yourself to move forward with a sense of lightness and renewed possibility. This process doesn't mean forgetting or condoning what happened; instead, it involves acknowledging the hurt, deciding to let it go, and consciously focusing on healing and growth.

Practicing self-forgiveness can be transformative, offering a pathway to self-acceptance and peace. Begin by reflecting on past actions and their impact, examining them honestly and with compassion. Acknowledge your mistakes and understand the context in which they occurred. This isn't about making excuses but about recognizing that everyone errs. This recognition is the first step toward self-forgiveness. Accept that you, like all humans, are flawed. Embrace these imperfections with self-compassion, reminding yourself that growth often emerges from missteps. As you practice self-forgiveness, consciously let go of the guilt and shame that may linger. Visualize these feelings as leaves carried away by a gentle stream, leaving behind a sense of calm and renewal.

Forgiving others who have caused harm requires empathy and understanding. Start by seeking to comprehend the reasons behind their actions. This doesn't mean excusing their behavior but recognizing that their actions may have stemmed from their own pain or struggles. By understanding, you can begin to release the anger and resentment that have taken hold. Holding onto these emotions only binds you to the past, preventing healing. Consider engaging in forgiveness rituals to find closure. This might involve writing a letter to the person who hurt you, expressing your feelings, and then choosing to forgive. You don't need to send the letter; writing can be cathartic. Meditation or visualization exercises can help you release grudges, envisioning them as balloons drifting away. You can even tie the letter to the balloon, watch it drift away, and actively feel the relief wash over you. Through these practices, you can focus on your healing and well-being.

Building a New Narrative

Everyone's life is like a book, with each chapter filled with experiences that have shaped who you are today. For many, these chapters are dominated by narratives written during times of pain, influenced by self-doubt and insecurity. Building a new narrative involves taking these stories and reframing them in a way that empowers and uplifts you. It's about transforming past experiences into sources of strength rather than anchors of despair. By actively rewriting your story, you create a positive self-image and envision a future where your past no longer dictates your present or future.

The first step in building a new narrative is identifying and challenging negative self-beliefs. These beliefs, often formed during childhood, can linger and warp your perception of yourself. Start by acknowledging these thoughts and questioning their validity. Ask yourself, "Is this belief based on fact, or is it a remnant of a past hurt?" Once identified, work on reframing past experiences to highlight resilience and growth. Instead of viewing setbacks as failures, see them as lessons contributing to your strength and wisdom. This mental shift empowers you to set positive intentions for the future, mapping out a life guided by hope and possibility rather than fear and doubt.

Ongoing self-reflection is vital in this process, contributing to continuous self-awareness and growth. Regular journaling allows you to track your progress, uncover patterns, and explore new insights about yourself. It serves as a mirror, reflecting your internal transformation and helping you stay aligned with your new narrative. Seeking feedback and support from trusted friends or mentors can also provide valuable perspectives, encouraging you to maintain momentum and challenging you to grow further. These relationships create a supportive network that reinforces your commitment to change.

Consider Sarah, who grew up believing she wasn't good enough. Through self-reflection and support from therapy, she reframed her childhood experiences, recognizing the resilience she developed under challenging times. By focusing on her strengths, Sarah built a narrative centered around her ability to overcome adversity, transforming self-doubt into confidence. Another individual, Michael, set positive intentions for his future by identifying his passions and pursuing them relentlessly. He used journaling to outline his goals, documenting his small victories, and adjusting his plans as needed. This process cultivated personal growth and opened doors to new opportunities and fulfillment.

As Chapter 7 draws to a close, it's clear that healing involves more than addressing past wounds; it requires crafting a new story of empowerment. By building a narrative that celebrates resilience and sets a hopeful path forward, you lay the groundwork for lasting change. As we move to the next chapter, remember that each step you take is a testament to your strength and potential.

"You don't have to see the whole staircase, just take the first step."

Martin Luther King Jr.

CHAPTER EIGHT

Improving Communication in Relationships

"Listen with curiosity. Speak with honesty. Act with integrity. The greatest problem with communication is we don't listen to understand. We listen to reply. When we listen with curiosity, we don't listen with the intent to reply. We listen for what's behind the words."

Roy T. Bennett, author

The Art of Non-Violent Communication (NVC)

You're having a conversation with your partner, and a misunderstanding spirals into a heated argument. Words are exchanged, but neither of you truly hears the other. This scenario is familiar to many, especially those navigating relationships with anxious attachment. Miscommunications can feel like quicksand, dragging you deeper into conflict with each misstep. Effective communication is the lifeline that can pull you out, promoting clarity, empathy, and connection.

One powerful approach to enhancing communication is Non-Violent Communication (NVC), a method developed by Marshall Rosenberg. NVC seeks to transform interactions by focusing on empathy and understanding rather than blame and judgment. It operates on four fundamental components: observations, feelings, needs, and requests. Observations involve describing what you see or hear objectively, without personal bias. This creates a shared reality, reducing misinterpretations. Feelings refer to the emotional responses tied to met or unmet needs. Expressing these emotions helps you take responsibility for your experience rather than projecting blame onto others. Needs are the universal desires at the core of human actions, such as safety, love, or respect. Identifying these needs allows for connection and cooperation. Finally, requests are the specific actions you propose to meet your needs, expressed as requests rather than demands, to encourage collaboration.

NVC offers numerous benefits for relationship dynamics. Reducing misunderstandings and conflicts paves the way for more harmonious interactions. The emphasis on empathy and connection encourages partners to see each other as allies rather than adversaries. This approach stimulates honest and respectful communication, where both parties feel heard and valued. As you practice NVC, you'll find that empathy becomes second nature, creating a more supportive and loving environment.

To practice NVC effectively, follow these steps: Begin with observations, stating what you notice without judgment. For instance, "I noticed you didn't call last night." Next, express your feelings without blame, such as "I felt worried." Then, identify your underlying needs, like "I need to know you're safe." Finally, make a clear and actionable request, such as "Can you call me if you're running late?" This structured approach minimizes defensiveness and enhances mutual understanding.

Consider a scenario where one partner interrupts the other during a conversation. Instead of reacting frustrated, NVC would guide you to say, "When you interrupt me, I feel frustrated because I need to be heard. Can we take turns speaking?" This method communicates your feelings, acknowledges the underlying need for respect, and proposes a constructive solution.

Interactive Element: NVC Practice Exercise

Reflect on a recent disagreement. Write down each side's observation, feeling, need, and request. Consider how using NVC might have changed the outcome. This exercise helps internalize the principles of NVC, making them more accessible during real-life interactions. Then, practice it with the next disagreement and witness the difference in the mood and outcome.

As you explore NVC, remember that it's a skill honed with practice. It requires patience and a willingness to see beyond immediate reactions to the deeper needs and emotions at play. By embracing this approach, you can transform your communication, creating a foundation of empathy and understanding.

Active Listening Skills for Better Understanding

Imagine a conversation where you feel truly heard. The other person is not just waiting for their turn to speak; they are fully present, absorbing your words and considering their meaning. This is the essence of active listening, a communication skill that goes beyond hearing to encompass truly understanding and thoughtfully responding. Active listening requires full attention, setting aside distractions, and focusing entirely on the speaker. It involves understanding verbal and non-verbal messages, ensuring you understand the entire context of what's being said. By avoiding interruptions and refraining from planning your response while the other person is speaking, you allow yourself to engage deeply with their message.

The benefits of active listening extend far beyond simply improving conversations. In relationships, it builds trust and respect, showing your partner or friend that you genuinely care about what they have to say. This creates a safe space for open communication, reducing misunderstandings that often lead to unnecessary conflict. As you practice active listening, emotional connections grow stronger. You become more attuned to the other person's needs and feelings, increasing empathy and understanding. This connection nurtures a sense of closeness and intimacy that can transform your interactions from mundane exchanges to meaningful dialogues.

There are several techniques you can use to enhance your active listening skills. Reflective listening is a powerful method of paraphrasing the speaker's words, confirming your understanding, and showing that you are engaged. For example, if your partner mentions feeling stressed about work, you might respond, "So you're feeling overwhelmed with your current workload?" This demonstrates that you are listening and gives them a chance to clarify or expand on their thoughts. Asking open-ended questions is another effective technique. These questions invite the speaker to share more, encouraging a deeper discussion. Instead of asking, "Did you have a good day?" try "What was the most interesting part of your day?" This way, you open the door to a richer conversation.

Non-verbal cues, such as nodding or making eye contact, play a crucial role in active listening. These signals show that you are present and attentive, reinforcing the speaker's sense that their words matter. Summarizing key points at the end of a discussion can also be beneficial. By recapping the main ideas, you ensure mutual understanding and provide closure to the conversation.

Consider practical exercises such as role-playing conversations with a partner to develop these skills. This allows you to practice reflective listening in a controlled setting, where both parties know the goal is to enhance communication. Another helpful exercise is to keep a listening journal. After conversations, jot down your reflections on how well you listened, noting areas for improvement. This self-awareness can help you track your progress and identify the best techniques for you. The power of active listening lies in its ability to transform how you connect with others, turning everyday conversations into opportunities for deeper understanding and connection.

"Excellent communication doesn't just happen natu-rally. It is a product of process, skill, climate, relation-ship and hard work."

Pat McMillan, author, CEO

Expressing Your Needs Without Fear

"I learned that courage was not the absence of fear, but the triumph over it. The brave man is not he who does not feel afraid, but he who conquers that fear."

Nelson Mandela

In any relationship, effective communication is like the sturdy bridge that connects two islands, allowing for the free exchange of thoughts and emotions. It is crucial for building secure attachments where both partners feel understood and valued. Misunderstandings can fester without clear and open dialogue, leading to resentment and disconnection. When you express your needs openly, you prevent these misunderstandings from taking root. This proactive approach allows for mutual respect and understanding, essential ingredients for enhancing relationship satisfaction. By articulating your needs, you lay the groundwork for a partnership built on trust and shared goals rather than assumptions and unmet expectations.

Communicating your needs effectively begins with honing specific techniques. Active listening is a foundational skill, ensuring you fully engage with your partner's perspective before sharing your own. Additionally, giving and receiving feedback can transform how you interact. Constructive feedback allows for growth and adjustment, keeping the relationship dynamic and responsive. Engaging in open conversations about what you need from your partner helps illuminate the path toward mutual fulfillment. However, fear and anxiety can often stand in the way of expressing these needs. Overcoming this barrier requires building self-confidence and self-worth. Understanding that your needs are valid and important is the first step toward asserting them. Practicing assertiveness techniques can bolster your confidence. These techniques help you express your needs clearly and respectfully without being aggressive or passive. Reframing negative thoughts about expressing needs is also crucial. Instead of fearing rejection or judgment, view these conversations as opportunities for growth and deeper connection.

Empathy plays a pivotal role in effective communication. It allows you to step into your partner's shoes, understand their feelings and experiences, and create a deeper connection. Practicing empathetic listening means fully engaging with your partner's emotions, validating their experiences, and responding with compassion. This not only strengthens the bond but also makes it easier to express your own needs. When both partners feel heard and understood, communicating needs becomes a collaborative effort rather than a confrontation.

To express your needs clearly and respectfully, use "I" statements. These phrases focus on your feelings and needs without blaming your partner. For example, "I need more quality time with you" is more effective than "You never spend time with me." Being specific and direct helps avoid ambiguity, ensuring your partner understands exactly what you are asking for. Keep the focus on personal needs rather than pointing fingers, which can trigger defensiveness. Timing and setting are also crucial. Choose a calm moment when both of you are relaxed and open to discussion rather than during a heated argument.

Consider these scenarios: You might say, "I feel overwhelmed when the house is messy. Can we create a cleaning schedule together?" This script not only expresses your need for order but also invites collaboration. Another example could be, "I need more quality time with you. Can we plan a date night this weekend?" Here, you clearly state your desire for connection and propose a solution, making it easier for your partner to respond positively. Adopting these communication techniques paves the way for more fulfilling and harmonious relationships.

Communicating During Conflict: Staying Calm and Clear

Conflict in relationships is inevitable, but it's also a natural part of being close to someone. The challenge in conflict lies not in the disagreement itself but in how you handle it. How it gets dealt with will either fortify the relationship or slowly erode it. Effective conflict resolution is crucial for maintaining emotional safety between partners. When emotions run high, stress levels rise, making communication increasingly difficult. Misunderstandings can quickly escalate, turning minor disagreements into major disputes, leaving scars, and creating resentment and distance over time. It's during these moments that maintaining respect and clarity becomes paramount. The goal is to navigate the choppy waters of conflict without capsizing the entire relationship. Effective communication in such situations helps resolve the immediate issue and strengthens the bond by promoting trust and understanding.

To keep calm during conflicts, start with deep breathing exercises. This simple technique helps to regulate your emotions, allowing you to think more clearly. Taking slow, deep breaths sends signals to your brain to relax, reducing the physiological symptoms of stress. Grounding exercises can also be beneficial. Focusing on physical sensations, like the feeling of your feet on the ground, can help anchor you to the present, preventing your mind from spiraling into panic. If the situation becomes overwhelming, don't hesitate to take a break. Stepping away for a few moments allows both partners to cool down and gather their thoughts, making it easier to return to the conversation with a clearer perspective and a calmer demeanor. Taking a break allows both of you to cool down, preventing further escalation and giving you time to reflect. This doesn't mean avoiding the issue but instead returning to it with a clearer mind and a calmer heart. When both partners agree to a temporary pause, it demonstrates a mutual commitment to resolving the conflict healthily. Upon returning to the discussion, the atmosphere is more conducive to finding a resolution.

Maintaining a calm and steady tone is equally important. How you say something can be just as impactful as what you say. A calm tone conveys respect and openness, reducing the likelihood of defensiveness. When expressing your feelings and needs, use "I" statements. This approach focuses on your own experiences rather than blaming your partner, reducing defensiveness and opening the path for genuine dialogue. For instance, saying, "I feel worried when you don't call," is more effective than "You never call when you're supposed to." Avoid accusations and blame, which only serve to escalate the conflict. Instead, aim to listen actively and empathetically to understand your partner's perspective. Listen to your partner's perspective thoroughly before responding, acknowledging their feelings, and showing that you value their viewpoint. Seek common ground and solutions rather than dwelling on the problem. This collaborative approach cultivates a sense of teamwork, turning the conflict into an opportunity for growth rather than a battleground.

Compromise and negotiation are the cornerstones of resolving conflicts. It's about finding solutions that satisfy both parties, even if it means meeting halfway. This requires identifying common goals and interests, which can redirect the focus from the conflict to the shared values and desires underlying it. Flexibility is key here. Being willing to adjust your stance and expecting the same from your partner can lead to agreeable outcomes. This practice not only resolves the immediate issue but also builds a sense of teamwork and collaboration, enhancing the relationship's overall resilience.

Role-playing exercises can be a valuable tool in practicing these communication skills. Consider a scenario where you feel anxious when your partner doesn't check in. During a mock argument, practice saying, "When you don't call, I feel worried because I care about your safety. Can we agree on a plan for checking in?" This exercise helps you express your feelings clearly and encourages your partner to respond constructively. During such exercises, active listening and reflective responses can significantly improve your ability to communicate effectively during actual conflicts. By simulating these scenarios, you build the skills needed to navigate the complexities of conflict with calmness and clarity.

As you navigate through conflicts, remember that each resolution is an opportunity to learn more about your partner and yourself. The skills you develop in resolving conflicts will serve as the foundation for a healthier, more connected relationship. In the next chapter, we will explore enhancing relationships further, building on the communication strategies and conflict resolution techniques covered here.

CHAPTER NINE

Enhancing Relationships

Building Trust Through Honest Communication

I magine sitting across from your partner, a warm cup of tea in your hands, feeling the comfort of their presence. This moment is serene, but it wasn't always this way. There were times when misunderstandings turned into arguments when words felt like walls instead of bridges. Building trust through honest communication is the key to transforming these moments of tension into opportunities for a deeper connection. Communication is not just about exchanging words; it's about sharing your truth in a way that invites understanding and empathy. As you navigate the complexities of relationships, remember this quote: "Communication is to relationships what breathing is to living." It is the lifeline that keeps love alive, allowing you to express your needs, fears, and dreams openly.

Trust is the bedrock of any relationship, the silent promise that assures both partners feel safe and valued. It is the cornerstone of emotional safety, allowing you to be your authentic self without fear of judgment or rejection. When trust is present, it stabilizes the relationship, allowing for emotional security. This security builds a foundation for relationship satisfaction and stability. The quiet strength holds relationships together, giving you the confidence to face challenges together. Trust ensures that when you fall, there is someone to catch you and stand by you through life's storms. This stability is not just comforting; it is the foundation upon which love and partnership thrive.

Building trust requires intentional effort and consistency. It begins with being true to your word. Consistency in actions and words is crucial; it shows your partner they can rely on you. If you say you will do something, follow through. This might seem simple, but it is powerful. Transparency and honesty are equally important. Open communication about your thoughts and feelings creates a space where trust can grow. Share your fears, dreams, and uncertainties without holding back. This vulnerability makes you grow closer, reinforcing the bond you share. Keeping promises is another pillar of trust. When you make a commitment, honor it. These actions, though small, accumulate over time, weaving a tapestry of reliability and faith that strengthens the relationship at its core.

However, trust is not given; it is earned through consistency and transparency. Rebuilding trust after a breach is challenging but not impossible. It requires courage and humility to acknowledge and take responsibility for mistakes. This acknowledgment is the first step toward healing, signaling your commitment to change. Engaging in open and honest discussions about the breach is essential. These conversations can be uncomfortable but necessary for understanding and resolution. Both partners must be willing to listen and express their feelings without defensiveness. It is through these dialogues that understanding and empathy can flourish. Offering and accepting sincere apologies is crucial. An apology is more than words; it is a promise to do better, to learn from the past, and to rebuild what was broken. This process involves patience and understanding from both partners, as healing takes time.

Once trust is broken, it can leave deep scars, but with effort and dedication, it can be mended. There may be hurdles in rebuilding, but each step taken together strengthens the partnership. Rebuilding trust is transformative, deepening the relationship and proving that love can endure even the toughest challenges. In this journey, remember that trust is not a destination but a continuous practice and commitment to nurturing the bond you share. As you navigate this path, keep in mind that trust is a gift you give to each other, a testament to the strength and resilience of your relationship.

Seeking Healthy Reassurance

Seeking reassurance in a relationship is natural, especially when you feel anxious or insecure. It is a natural expression of vulnerability. It's a way to affirm that you are valued, heard, and understood. There's a delicate balance between seeking reassurance and becoming dependent on it. As the saying goes, "It's not the asking for reassurance that's the issue; it's how we ask and what we do with it that makes the difference." When reassurance becomes a constant need, it can strain relationships, creating a dynamic where one partner feels burdened by the other's insecurities. Healthy reassurance involves open communication about your needs and understanding your partner's perspective. It means expressing your feelings without placing blame and seeking reassurance without demanding constant validation. Doing so creates a dynamic where both partners feel valued and heard. It's essential to recognize that reassurance, when done healthily, can strengthen bonds, ensuring a sense of shared understanding and empathy between partners.

Seeking reassurance in a way that supports rather than undermines your relationship is essential to communicating openly about your needs. Start by expressing your feelings clearly and without blame. Instead of saying, "You never show you care," try, "I feel a bit insecure right now and could use some reassurance." This invites your partner into your emotional world without putting them on the defensive. It's crucial to understand that reassurance is not about demanding validation but seeking a connection that nurtures both partners. Expressing your needs with honesty and respect encourages your partner to do the same, creating a dynamic of mutual support.

Equally important is the way you respond to reassurance. When your partner offers support, take it in fully. Reflect on their words and let them reinforce your sense of security. Avoid the temptation to dismiss their reassurances or to seek more immediately.

Instead, remind yourself of the trust and love that fortifies their words. Practicing self-soothing techniques can also help manage the anxiety that often drives the need for reassurance. Techniques such as deep breathing, mindfulness, or even taking a short walk can provide the space to process your emotions and reduce the intensity of your insecurities.

Consider the story of Emily and Jake. Emily often felt anxious about her relationship, frequently seeking reassurance from Jake. Initially, this created tension, as Jake felt overwhelmed by her constant need for validation. After discussing their feelings openly, Emily learned to articulate her needs more clearly, while Jake practiced offering reassurance without feeling pressured. They found that working together could meet each other's emotional needs without compromising their independence. This shift allowed them to build a relationship where reassurance was a source of strength rather than a point of contention.

Incorporating these approaches can transform how reassurance functions in your relationship. It becomes a bridge that connects rather than a crutch that divides. By seeking reassurance with intention and responding with gratitude, you and your partner can navigate the complexities of your emotional landscape together, creating a resilient and nurturing relationship.

Overcoming Fear of Intimacy

"The best way to deal with relationship anxiety is by being honest, open, and understanding with your partner — these qualities will go a long way in helping you both overcome any fears or insecurities together."

Dr. Sue Johnson

Fear of intimacy often begins with past experiences that leave deep emotional scars. For many with anxious attachment, the roots of this fear lie in memories of rejection and abandonment. When early caregivers were inconsistent or emotionally unavailable, the message received was that vulnerability could lead to pain. This creates a fear of letting others in, as the emotional exposure risk is too high. The vulnerability required in intimate relationships often triggers anxiety, as it opens the door to potential hurt. The mind, conditioned by past betrayals, becomes wary of closeness, creating a reluctance to engage in emotional intimacy fully. This fear can manifest in various ways, such as avoiding deep conversations, shying away from physical closeness, or even self-sabotaging relationships before they become too serious. The cycle of withdrawal and self-protection becomes a barrier to forming meaningful connections.

Vital to overcoming this fear is to take gradual steps toward embracing intimacy. Start with small, low-risk acts that build confidence. This might be sharing a personal story with a friend or expressing a need in a relationship. These small steps help you become more comfortable with vulnerability. As you build confidence, gradually increase your emotional disclosures. Share your fears, dreams, and insecurities with trusted individuals. This practice nurtures a sense of safety and demonstrates that vulnerability can lead to deeper connections. Practice self-soothing techniques to manage anxiety, reminding yourself that vulnerability is a strength, not a weakness. When feelings of fear arise, practice deep breathing, mindfulness, or positive affirmations to ground yourself. These techniques help regulate emotional responses and reinforce the belief that intimacy is not something to fear but to embrace.

The benefits of overcoming the fear of intimacy are profound. Embracing closeness leads to deeper emotional connections as you allow others to see your true self. This authenticity allows for trust and mutual understanding, enhancing relationship satisfaction. As you open up, you invite others to do the same, creating a reciprocal dynamic of sharing and support. An increased sense of security emerges as you realize that vulnerability does not equate to weakness. Instead, it becomes a source of strength, reinforcing your self-worth and confidence. Relationships become more prosperous and more fulfilling as the barriers that once held you back begin to dissolve. This transformation extends beyond personal relationships, influencing how you engage with the world. The fear that once dictated your interactions is replaced by a newfound assurance, allowing you to cultivate meaningful connections and live authentically.

Creating Emotional Safety

Emotional safety is the feeling that you can be your true self without fear of judgment or rejection and is the foundation upon which healthy relationships are built. It is the assurance that you can express your true self without fear of judgment or rejection. When emotional safety is present, trust and intimacy flourish, allowing both partners to feel understood and accepted. This safety is a buffer against misunderstandings, creating a stable and satisfying relationship. It provides a space for welcoming and celebrating vulnerability, encouraging deeper connections and mutual growth. In such an environment, partners can share thoughts and feelings openly, knowing their emotions will be met with empathy and support. This creates a dynamic where each person feels valued and cherished, strengthening their bond.

Consistent and non-judgmental communication is vital to creating and maintaining emotional safety. This means actively listening to your partner without rushing to conclusions or judgments. By approaching conversations with an open mind and heart, you create a space where both partners can express themselves freely. Empathy and validation play a crucial role in this process. When your partner shares their feelings, acknowledge their emotions and show understanding. This doesn't mean you have to agree with everything they say, but it does require recognizing their perspective as valid. Setting and respecting boundaries is another vital step. Boundaries are not meant to create distance but to define a safe space where both partners feel comfortable. Discuss and agree on boundaries together, ensuring they reflect the needs and values of both individuals. This mutual respect will create an environment where emotional safety can thrive.

Maintaining emotional safety is challenging. Personal triggers and past traumas can resurface, threatening the sense of security within the relationship. It's important to recognize these triggers and communicate them to your partner. You invite your partner to understand and support you by sharing your vulnerabilities. Navigating differences in communication styles can also be an obstacle. Some people are more expressive, while others may struggle to articulate their feelings. Patience and adaptability are crucial here. Take the time to learn each other's communication preferences and adapt your approach accordingly. This requires effort and willingness to compromise but ultimately strengthens the relationship. When conflicts arise, approach them as opportunities for growth rather than threats to safety. Address issues calmly and constructively, focusing on finding solutions rather than assigning blame. This mindset encourages a culture of safety and mutual respect, reinforcing the emotional bond.

Creating emotional safety is an ongoing process that requires commitment from both partners. It's about nurturing a relationship where both individuals feel secure, valued, and loved. As you continue to foster this safety, you will likely find that your relationship becomes more resilient, able to withstand the challenges that life inevitably brings. In this secure environment, intimacy deepens, and the connection between partners grows more substantial, creating a fulfilling and enduring relationship.

Supporting Each Other's Growth

In relationships, the role of mutual support is vital. It is the nurturing soil in which both personal and relational growth flourish. When you support each other's growth, you're not just investing in the individual; you're enriching the fabric of your relationship. Encouraging personal goals and aspirations fuels a sense of achievement and fulfillment for each partner. This, in turn, spills over into the relationship, creating a dynamic where both individuals feel valued and understood. You forge stronger bonds by engaging in shared activities and interests, deepening your connection through shared experiences. Providing emotional and practical support cements this foundation, ensuring both partners feel equipped to pursue their dreams confidently. This mutual backing creates a relationship where growth is both a shared and individual pursuit, enhancing satisfaction and stability.

Supporting each other's growth can, however, come with challenges. Balancing personal and relationship needs requires careful navigation. It's essential to recognize that while the relationship is a partnership, each person has unique aspirations that need nurturing. There may be times when your paths diverge, and that's okay. The key is communicating openly about these differences, ensuring both partners feel heard and respected. Navigating differing goals and aspirations demands flexibility and understanding. It's about finding common ground where both individual and shared dreams can coexist. This balance is not always easy to achieve, but with patience and empathy, it is possible to support each other's growth without compromising personal ambitions.

Consider the story of Alex and Sam, a couple who beautifully exemplify mutual support. Alex had always dreamt of pursuing a photography career, while Sam wanted to complete a marathon. Instead of viewing these goals as separate endeavors, they found ways to support each other. Alex attended Sam's training sessions, cheering him on and providing motivation. Meanwhile, Sam helped Alex set up photo shoots, offering constructive feedback and encouragement. Through these acts of support, they achieved their individual goals and strengthened their bond. Their story illustrates that when partners encourage each other's personal goals, they create a relationship that thrives on shared successes and mutual admiration.

Another example is Emma and Leo, who discovered the power of engaging in shared activities. They took up hiking as a hobby, exploring new trails together every weekend. This shared interest became a cornerstone of their relationship, allowing them to connect, communicate, and support each other in a relaxed setting. Their hikes were not just about reaching the summit but about the conversations and camaraderie along the way. This mutual engagement strengthened their relationship, proving that shared activities can be a powerful tool for connection and growth.

CHAPTER TEN

Building Secure Attachments

What is a Secure Attachment?

Picture yourself standing on a beach, watching the waves gently lap at the shore. Each wave is consistent, predictable, and soothing, much like the foundations of a secure attachment. In the realm of relationships, secure attachment resembles this tranquil scene, embodying trust, stability, and emotional equilibrium. Unlike the turbulent waters of anxious attachment, where emotions surge unpredictably, secure attachment provides a calming presence, offering a sense of safety and comfort in the relationships you cherish.

A secure attachment is characterized by feeling safe and at ease in relationships. It is the ability to trust your partner and be trustworthy in return. Emotional regulation becomes second nature; you manage your feelings effectively, responding to challenges with calmness rather than chaos. There's a healthy balance between independence and interdependence, where you enjoy time alone and cherish moments with your loved ones. This balance creates a space where both partners can thrive, individually and together, without fearing losing themselves or each other. Emotional stability and trust are the cornerstones of secure attachment, allowing you to navigate life's ups and downs with confidence and poise.

The benefits of developing a secure attachment are profound. Relationship satisfaction improves as you and your partner communicate openly, resolving conflicts with empathy and understanding. Emotional regulation becomes more refined, reducing the emotional rollercoaster often accompanying anxious attachment. You cultivate a greater sense of personal security and self-worth, no longer relying on external validation to feel whole. Resilience to stress increases, enabling you to face challenges with grace and determination. Secure attachment nurtures an environment where love thrives and personal growth flourishes, unencumbered by the shadows of doubt and fear.

Secure attachment brings stable self-esteem, where you know you're worth inherently. Trust becomes a guiding principle, enabling you to believe in your partner's intentions and your own capabilities. Emotional regulation replaces turmoil, allowing consistent and measured responses to life's challenges.

Characteristic behaviors of a secure attachment include the ability to trust your partners and feel comfortable with independence. Healthy communication patterns emerge, where you express needs and listen empathetically. Emotions remain consistent, not swayed by fleeting doubts or fears. You feel empowered to explore your individuality while maintaining a solid connection with your partner. These behaviors create a foundation for enduring love and mutual respect, creating nurturing and liberating relationships.

It's important to know that transitioning from anxious to secure attachment is entirely possible. It requires effort and persistence, but the rewards are immeasurable. Consider stories of individuals who have successfully transitioned, embracing a new way of relating to themselves and others. With dedication and the right tools, you can cultivate secure attachment, transforming your relationships and your life in ways you only imagined.

Steps to Transition from Anxious to Secure Attachment

Imagine waking up daily with a newfound sense of calm, knowing you can confidently face challenges. This shift begins with adopting a growth mindset, where you see difficulties not as insurmountable obstacles but as opportunities for growth. This mindset encourages you to reframe negative thoughts about self-worth, replacing them with affirmations of your inherent value. By viewing setbacks as learning experiences, you build resilience and lay the groundwork for secure attachment.

To develop secure attachment behaviors, start by enhancing your self-awareness and emotional regulation. This involves recognizing your emotional triggers and learning to manage them effectively. Building trust in relationships requires consistent actions that demonstrate reliability and dependability. Engage in open and honest communication, expressing your needs and listening empathetically to your partner. These foundational steps create a stable environment where you and your partner can thrive.

Practical steps to facilitate this transition include identifying and challenging anxious thoughts. When you notice a negative thought pattern, question its validity and consider alternative perspectives. Practicing self-compassion and self-care is crucial; it strengthens your self-worth and reinforces the belief that you deserve love and respect. Establish and maintain healthy boundaries to protect your emotional well-being and have mutual respect in relationships.

Self-care plays a pivotal role in developing secure attachments. Establish a self-care routine encompassing physical, emotional, and mental health practices. This could include regular exercise, mindfulness meditation, and nurturing hobbies. Self-compassion is equally essential; treating yourself with kindness and understanding builds self-worth and resilience.

Incorporate practical exercises into your daily life to reinforce secure attachment behaviors. Engage in trust-building exercises with your partner, such as shared activities that require collaboration and communication. Use journaling prompts to reflect on your progress and identify areas for growth. Daily affirmations can help cultivate a secure mindset, grounding you in positive self-beliefs.

Consistency is key. Regular mindfulness practice, daily affirmations, and journaling for self-reflection can support secure attachment. Long-term strategies like ongoing therapy or counseling, joining support groups, and committing to personal development reinforce this transformation, ensuring a lasting foundation for healthy, secure relationships.

Building Trust in Yourself and Others

"Trust is built with consistency."

Lincoln Chafee

Imagine trusting yourself as effortlessly as you trust the ground beneath your feet. Self-trust forms the foundation of all other relationships, yet it's often overlooked. Building it starts with keeping promises to yourself. Whether waking up early for a morning jog or taking time to read, honoring these commitments strengthens your confidence in your abilities. Each promise kept is a testament to your reliability. Listening to your needs is equally important. This means respecting your limits and acknowledging when you need rest or support. Reflect on past successes, no matter how small, as they remind you of your capabilities and resilience. These reflections are not mere nostalgia but reinforcements of your inherent worth, guiding you to make choices aligned with your true self.

In relationships, trust is the glue that binds two people together. Open and honest communication is its backbone, allowing partners to express their thoughts and feelings without fear of judgment or misunderstanding. Reliability and consistency are crucial; showing up when expected and keeping your word builds a sense of security. Everyone makes mistakes, but learning to forgive them and grow from experiences creates a deeper connection. This doesn't mean forgetting but understanding and moving forward together, stronger than before.

To cultivate trust, consider engaging in trust journaling, where you record instances of trust and reliability in your life. This practice highlights patterns and areas for improvement. Partner trust exercises can enhance mutual trust, such as shared activities that require cooperation. These exercises create opportunities for vulnerability, where partners learn to rely on each other. Self-reflection questions about trust can deepen your understanding of its role in your life. Ask yourself how trust has shaped your experiences and what it means to you. These exercises are not just tasks but gateways to building a more trusting and fulfilling relationship with yourself and others.

Gradual Exposure to Vulnerability

Imagine standing at the edge of a pool, hesitating to dive into the water's unknown embrace. Vulnerability feels much the same—daunting yet necessary for deep emotional connections. It builds trust and intimacy, the lifeblood of secure attachments. Without vulnerability, relationships remain superficial, lacking the depth that comes from shared fears and hopes. Being vulnerable means showing your true self, risking rejection, and facing judgment. Yet, this very openness allows partners to truly see and accept each other, creating a profound sense of belonging and understanding.

To become more comfortable with vulnerability, start small. Begin with low-risk disclosures, like sharing a personal interest or a minor concern. As you grow more at ease, gradually increase the level of personal information shared. Discuss a past experience that shaped you or a fear that lingers. Practicing this in safe and supportive environments is important—perhaps with a trusted friend or partner who values genuine connection. These interactions serve as a rehearsal for more extensive, more significant revelations, building your confidence to open up further.

Embracing vulnerability brings numerous benefits, transforming how you relate to others and yourself. You forge deeper emotional connections with partners as they learn to appreciate the authentic you. The walls that once separated you crumble, replaced by bridges of understanding and empathy. This openness increases the sense of security, knowing you are valued for who you truly are. Self-acceptance blossoms as vulnerability reveals the beauty in flaws and the strength in honesty. With each step you take into the pool of vulnerability, you discover that the water is warm and the swim is liberating.

Setting Healthy Boundaries

A beautiful garden, flourishing with vibrant flowers and lush greenery, is surrounded by a sturdy fence representing healthy boundaries, essential for nurturing relationships and personal well-being. Healthy boundaries define where you end, and others begin, protecting your emotional space while allowing genuine connection. They provide safety, ensuring your needs and limits are respected, and you can interact authentically with others. Unhealthy boundaries, in contrast, might resemble a garden overrun with weeds or enclosed by walls too high for light to enter—either too porous or too rigid, leading to confusion and resentment.

Establishing and maintaining healthy boundaries requires careful consideration and consistency. Begin by identifying your personal limits and needs. Reflect on what makes you feel comfortable or uncomfortable in interactions. Once these are clear, communicate your boundaries assertively yet calmly. Use "I" statements to express your needs without blaming others. For example, say, "I need time alone to recharge," rather than, "You make me feel overwhelmed." Practicing consistency in enforcing these boundaries is crucial. If you waver, it sends mixed signals, making it difficult for others to respect your needs.

Challenges inevitably arise when setting boundaries. Fear of rejection or conflict can make it hard to assert your needs. You might worry about how others will react or fear damaging relationships. Saying no can feel uncomfortable, especially if you're used to prioritizing others' needs over your own. However, remember that boundaries are not walls but guidelines for healthy interactions. Overcoming these fears involves recognizing that genuine respect and understanding come from clear communication. When you articulate your boundaries, you teach others how to treat you, creating respect and trust.

Consider the story of Mia, who realized her friendships were draining her. She began setting clear boundaries, communicating her need for space without guilt. Her friends initially struggled but eventually respected her needs, leading to more fulfilling interactions. Another couple, Alex and Jordan, strengthened their relationship by setting mutual boundaries around work-life balance. They agreed on dedicated times for connection, improving their relationship satisfaction. These examples highlight the transformative power of boundaries in enhancing relationships and personal well-being.

Developing Emotional Resilience

"A good half of the art of living is resilience."
Alain de Botton

Emotional resilience is like a sturdy bridge that connects you to your ability to withstand life's inevitable challenges. It allows you to bounce back from adversity, maintaining your balance even when the ground beneath you shifts. Imagine facing a storm not with dread but with the confidence that you have the tools to weather it. This reminds me of my favorite quote: "Life isn't about waiting for the storm to pass. It's about learning how to dance in the rain." This resilience enables you to manage stress and emotions effectively, transforming potential setbacks into opportunities for growth. It nurtures a positive outlook, guiding you to see beyond immediate struggles and envision brighter possibilities. Cultivating this resilience is crucial for fostering secure attachments, as it provides the emotional stability needed to navigate the complexities of relationships with grace and strength.

Building emotional resilience involves practical techniques that can be incorporated into your daily life. Practicing gratitude is a powerful method, helping you focus on the positives amidst chaos. By regularly acknowledging and appreciating the good in your life, you train your mind to seek out joy and contentment. Developing problem-solving skills further enhances resilience, equipping you to approach challenges with a solution-oriented mindset. This proactive approach shifts your focus from obstacles to opportunities, empowering you to tackle difficulties head-on. Regular physical activity also plays a significant role in bolstering resilience. Exercise releases endorphins, those feel-good hormones that naturally elevate your mood and reduce stress, while building physical strength reinforces mental toughness.

Specific exercises can help enhance your resilience. Gratitude journaling is a simple yet transformative practice. By recording daily gratitudes, you create a tangible reminder of the positivity in your life, reinforcing your capacity to overcome challenges. Engaging in problem-solving scenarios allows you to practice solving hypothetical challenges, honing your critical thinking and adaptability. Physical resilience activities, like regular exercise routines, strengthen your body and fortify your mind, creating a foundation of resilience that supports your emotional and physical well-being. These practices interweave to build a resilient mindset, ready to face life's uncertainties with confidence and strength.

Cultivating Healthy Relationship Habits

In the tapestry of life, relationships form the vibrant threads that weave together our experiences, emotions, and aspirations. Healthy relationship habits act as the loom, aligning these threads into a cohesive and harmonious pattern. At their core, these habits encompass regular communication, mutual respect, and balanced time together and apart. Open communication is the bridge between partners, allowing for the free flow of thoughts and feelings without fear of judgment. Mutual respect underpins this dialogue, acknowledging each partner's individuality and fostering an environment of support. Relationships thrive when partners balance shared moments and individual pursuits, ensuring that time spent apart strengthens the bond rather than weakens it. Shared goals and values further cement this foundation, providing a common direction and purpose that guides the relationship forward.

To cultivate these habits, begin by setting regular check-ins with your partner. These moments of connection can be as simple as a weekly coffee date or a nightly walk. During these check-ins, practice active listening, focusing entirely on your partner's words, seeking to understand rather than respond. Support each other's interests and goals by celebrating successes and offering encouragement during challenges. These actions demonstrate investment in each other's growth and happiness, reinforcing the partnership's strength. Doing so will help relationships find the nourishment needed to flourish amidst life's demands.

Consider the story of Laura and James, who transformed their relationship by dedicating one evening a week to a date night. This ritual became a sanctuary where they could reconnect, free from the distractions of daily life. My husband and I will allow for a weekly check-in where we discuss and come to any conclusion needed together. This allows for a healthy relationship and ensures we stay aligned with each other and our aspirations. These examples illustrate the power of intentional habits in creating a resilient and joyful relationship.

To facilitate these practices, engage in exercises and activities designed to strengthen your bond. Use relationship check-in templates to guide your discussions, ensuring you cover essential topics while allowing space for spontaneity. Shared goal-setting worksheets can help you outline and prioritize your aspirations, providing a roadmap for your collective journey. Active listening practice sessions can deepen your empathy and understanding, transforming how you engage with each other. Through these exercises, you cultivate a relationship that is not only enduring but also deeply fulfilling.

Maintaining Security in Relationships

A garden will only flourish if tended to regularly; the same goes for having a secure relationship. Building secure attachments isn't a destination; it's an ongoing process requiring continuous care. Regular self-reflection and open communication are vital, serving as the sunlight and water that nurture growth. By routinely evaluating your emotions and interactions, you gain insights into your needs and your partner's, ensuring alignment and understanding. Communication acts as a bridge, allowing both partners to express thoughts and resolve misunderstandings, creating a foundation of trust and security.

Mutual support and understanding play a crucial role in maintaining this security. Supporting each other's personal growth and goals is like providing nourishment for the garden encouraging each plant to thrive. Engage in shared activities and experiences that nurture connection and mutual appreciation. Whether taking a class together or exploring new hobbies, these shared moments strengthen your bond and reinforce your commitment to each other's happiness.

Incorporating practical strategies can further secure your relationship. Regular relationship check-ins offer a dedicated time to discuss feelings, celebrate successes, and address any concerns. Practicing gratitude and appreciation for each other enhances emotional intimacy, reminding you of the value you bring to each other's lives. For example, I constantly tell my husband I am grateful for what he has done for me or our family. He returns the favor, creating mutual gratitude, and nothing "small" goes unnoticed. Continued engagement in self-care and emotional regulation practices also ensures that both partners maintain their well-being, contributing to a stable and supportive environment.

The importance of mutual growth cannot be overstated. As individuals evolve, so must the relationship. Encourage each other's aspirations and provide the support needed to achieve personal goals. This mutual investment in growth creates a dynamic relationship that adapts to life's changes and is ready to face challenges with resilience and unity. Each step taken together strengthens the foundation, ensuring the garden of your relationship remains lush and vibrant.

As we conclude this chapter, remember that maintaining security in relationships is an active process of nurturing and growth, like tending to a garden. With dedication and care, you can cultivate an enduring and deeply rewarding partnership.

CHAPTER ELEVEN

Long-Term Strategies for Lasting Change

Maintaining Your Progress: Consistency is Key

"Success isn't always about greatness. It's about consistency. Consistent hard work leads to success. Greatness will come."

Dwayne Johnson

At first, a jigsaw puzzle seems daunting, with pieces scattered across the table. But with time and patience, you begin to recognize the patterns, slowly building the picture you envision. This is much like the process of creating lasting change in your life. Each piece you fit together represents a new habit, a small victory, a step toward your desired life. Consistency is the glue that holds these pieces together, transforming a collection of parts into a coherent whole. As you embark on this chapter, think of consistency as your steadfast companion, helping you maintain progress and navigate the challenges of change.

Maintaining consistency is crucial in reinforcing new habits and behaviors. Like a steady drumbeat, it keeps you on track and prevents you from slipping back into old patterns. When you consistently practice new skills, they become second nature, seamlessly integrating into your daily life. Consistency builds resilience, providing the confidence and strength to face obstacles without losing momentum. It helps you trust yourself, knowing you have the dedication to follow through. As you embrace this consistency, you create a foundation of stability that supports your growth, much like a tree with solid roots weathering the storms.

To stay consistent, start by setting realistic and achievable goals. Break down larger objectives into manageable steps. This approach prevents you from being overwhelmed and allows you to celebrate small victories along the way. Creating a daily routine is another powerful strategy. A routine provides structure, minimizing decision fatigue and preserving mental energy for more significant challenges. As you adhere to your routine, you form habits that support your progress. Tracking your progress is equally important. Celebrate small wins, no matter how minor they seem, as they reinforce your commitment and motivate you to keep going.

Several tools can support your journey toward consistency. Habit-tracking apps visually represent your progress, allowing you to see patterns and identify areas for improvement. They serve as gentle reminders, nudging you to stay on course. Consider enlisting an accountability partner who encourages you and holds you responsible for your commitments. Regular self-assessment check-ins provide an opportunity to reflect on your journey, evaluate your progress, and make necessary adjustments. These tools act as safety nets, catching you when you falter and propelling you forward.

Despite your best efforts, challenges may arise that disrupt your consistency. Life is unpredictable, and setbacks are a natural part of the process. When faced with obstacles, approach them with flexibility and adaptability. Adjust your routines to accommodate changes in your circumstances while keeping your goals in sight. Seek additional support when needed, whether through a therapist, support group, or trusted friend. Remember that asking for help is a sign of strength, not weakness. Dealing with setbacks requires resilience. Instead of viewing them as failures, see them as opportunities for growth and learning. Reflect on what went wrong, identify lessons learned, and apply them to future efforts. I have had many setbacks that made me feel as if I was a failure and there was no reason to continue moving forward if I was going to fail again. During these moments, my support system aided me in realizing the only way you can fail yourself is by not getting back up and keep trying. I am by no means perfect, and I've learned that being "perfect" is impossible. You have to give yourself grace and stay consistent. The timeline you have in your head isn't accurate;

the reality is there is no one "right" or "straight" path. Your path is one of falling off the path and getting back up to keep moving forward. Consistency will get you there.

Interactive Element: Consistency Check-In

Take a moment to reflect on your current habits and routines. Identify an area where consistency has been a challenge. What are the roadblocks you've encountered? Write down one small, realistic step to improve consistency in this area. Set a date to review your progress and adjust your approach if needed. This check-in serves as a commitment to yourself, reinforcing your dedication to lasting change.

Building a Support System: Friends, Family, and Community

In the realm of emotional well-being, a robust support system acts as a crucial anchor, providing both the emotional and practical support needed to navigate life's challenges. Imagine how a network of roots supports a towering tree; your support system functions similarly, offering stability and strength. These connections enhance motivation and accountability, giving you the encouragement needed to pursue your goals and maintain your progress. They also reduce feelings of isolation and loneliness, allowing you to feel seen, heard, and valued. With a reliable support network, the weight of burdens is shared, making them easier to bear.

Building and maintaining supportive relationships starts with identifying trustworthy and empathetic individuals. These people listen without judgment and understand your struggles without minimizing them. Once identified, it's essential to communicate your needs and boundaries clearly. This might mean expressing yourself when you need space or company ensuring that your relationships remain healthy and balanced. Regularly connecting and spending time with these supportive individuals strengthens your bonds, reinforcing the foundation of your support network. Whether it's a weekly catch-up call or a monthly coffee date, these interactions nurture your connections, making them more resilient and enduring.

Expanding your support network can further enrich your life with diverse perspectives and experiences. Consider joining support groups or therapy groups where shared experiences foster understanding and camaraderie. Participating in community events or clubs can also introduce you to like-minded individuals who share your interests and values. Engaging in online support forums offers the flexibility to connect with others from the comfort of your home, providing a sense of community even from afar. These avenues open doors to new friendships, broadening your circle and enhancing your emotional support system.

Utilize your support group effectively to get the most out of your support network. Don't hesitate to ask for help when needed, recognizing that seeking support is a sign of strength, not weakness. In turn, offer your support to others, creating a reciprocal relationship where both parties benefit. Celebrating successes together, no matter how small, reinforces the bonds of your relationships, creating a sense of shared joy and accomplishment.

These practices ensure that your support system remains a dynamic and nurturing presence in your life.

Interactive Element: Building Your Support Network

Take a piece of paper and draw a circle in the center to represent yourself. Around it, draw smaller circles for each person in your current support system. Consider who supports you emotionally, practically, and socially. Reflect on the balance of giving and receiving support, and identify areas where your network could expand or strengthen. This exercise provides a visual representation of your support system, highlighting its strengths and growth areas.

Ongoing Self-Reflection and Personal Growth

Imagine looking into a mirror that reflects your physical appearance and the intricate tapestry of your thoughts, feelings, and aspirations. This is the power of self-reflection—a vital practice for anyone committed to personal growth. Regular self-reflection enhances your self-awareness, providing a clearer understanding of who you are and what drives you. It acts as a compass, guiding you toward areas requiring improvement. Through this reflective lens, you can identify habits and behaviors that no longer serve you, making space for positive changes that align with your core values.

Self-reflection is more than just a fleeting thought; it is a deliberate practice that requires commitment and structure. A reflection journal is one of the most effective ways to incorporate self-reflection into daily life. This journal becomes a personal sanctuary where you can explore your thoughts and emotions without judgment. Dedicate a few minutes each day to jot down your reflections, focusing on your experiences and any lessons learned. Over time, these entries will reveal patterns and insights, offering a roadmap for personal development. Additionally, setting aside time for weekly or monthly self-assessments can deepen your understanding of your progress. These assessments allow you to step back and evaluate your journey, recognizing accomplishments and areas needing attention.

For continuous personal growth, engage in activities that challenge and inspire you. Reading self-help and personal development books can offer fresh perspectives and practical strategies for overcoming obstacles. These texts serve as mentors, providing wisdom and guidance. Attending workshops, seminars, or retreats can also be transformative. These immersive experiences connect you with others on similar paths, creating a supportive environment for learning and growth. Engaging in new hobbies or learning new skills encourages you to step out of your comfort zone, allowing for creativity and resilience. Whether painting, dancing, or learning a new language, these activities stimulate your mind and enrich your life.

Setting personal growth goals is a powerful way to stay focused and motivated. Use the SMART criteria—Specific, Measurable, Achievable, Relevant, and Time-bound—to create clear and attainable goals. This structured approach ensures that your goals are not just dreams but actionable plans. Regularly revisiting and adjusting these goals is crucial. Life is dynamic, and your goals should reflect your evolving priorities and circumstances. Celebrate your achievements and milestones along the way, no matter how small. These celebrations recognize your efforts and reinforce your commitment to growth.

Self-reflection and personal growth are intertwined, each fueling the other in a continuous cycle of development. As you become more self-aware, you gain insights that inspire change, leading to personal and emotional evolution. This ongoing process requires dedication and patience, but the rewards are profound. By investing in self-reflection, you cultivate a deeper understanding of yourself, paving the way for a more fulfilling and authentic life. Through this practice, you enhance your personal growth and enrich your relationships and interactions with the world around you.

Creating a Daily Self-Care Routine

In the bustling rhythm of everyday life, self-care often takes a backseat. Yet, it acts as the backbone of emotional well-being, vital for maintaining the progress you've worked so hard to achieve. By nurturing your mental and emotional health, self-care provides a foundation of resilience and stability. It's like grounding yourself amidst the chaos, offering a moment of peace to recharge. When you prioritize self-care, you are essentially telling yourself that your needs matter. This practice sustains you through life's ups and downs and enhances your capacity to cope with challenges. For me, this was a hard one. I always correlated self-care with being selfish. It was as if sitting down and reading a book and not doing the housework was unthinkable. It took commitment and reshaping my mind to realize that self-care is NOT selfish. The way I could think about this, which made it seem more reasonable, was by looking at airplane safety videos. They say to put your mask on for oxygen flow before helping others, but that never resonated with me. Why would I help myself before someone else? After much deliberation, I realized that you can not help someone else if you are crumbling. Once this was a thought that I could grasp, self-care made so much sense. You are in charge of yourself, and if you don't care for yourself, how will you survive? This was a significant turning point in realizing that staying consistent about self-care would help me throughout my life.

Creating a personalized self-care routine begins with identifying activities that resonate with your personal needs. This is not a one-size-fits-all approach; what soothes one person may not work for another. Start by reflecting on what brings you joy and peace. Perhaps it's a morning walk that clears your mind or an evening spent reading your favorite book. Once you've identified these activities, schedule regular self-care time. Consider it a non-negotiable appointment with yourself, much like a meeting or a doctor's visit. Protect this time fiercely, and let it remind you of your commitment to your well-being.

Balancing different types of self-care is crucial. Physical self-care might include activities like yoga, which stretches your body and calms your mind, or a brisk walk that invigorates your senses. Emotional self-care could involve mindfulness practices or meditation, allowing you to sit with your thoughts without judgment.

Mental self-care might mean engaging in hobbies or creative pursuits, such as painting or playing an instrument. These activities stimulate your mind, offering a break from routine and sparking joy. Incorporating various self-care practices creates a holistic routine that nurtures every aspect of your being.

Mindfulness and meditation are powerful tools in your self-care arsenal. They teach you to be present, focusing on the here and now rather than dwelling on the past or worrying about the future. Even a few minutes daily can make a significant difference, grounding you and reducing stress. Physical activities like yoga or walking offer similar benefits. They connect you with your body, releasing endorphins that elevate your mood. Whether the gentle flow of a yoga sequence or the rhythmic pace of a walk, these activities create a sense of harmony between body and mind.

Engaging in hobbies and creative pursuits is another enriching form of self-care. These activities provide an outlet for self-expression and creativity, allowing you to explore new facets of yourself. Whether painting, writing, or gardening, find something that excites you and dedicate time to it regularly. These moments of creativity can be incredibly therapeutic, offering a break from the demands of daily life and a chance to recharge.

In weaving these practices into your daily life, you create a self-care routine that supports your ongoing healing and emotional well-being. This routine becomes a sanctuary, a place where you can retreat and find solace amidst the noise of the world. As you nurture this routine, it will, in turn, encourage you, providing the strength and resilience needed to face life's challenges. Embrace self-care as an integral part of your journey, enriching your life and supporting your growth.

By cultivating a self-care routine, you lay the groundwork for lasting change, reinforcing your progress. As you continue to explore these practices, remember that self-care is not a luxury but a necessity. It is an ongoing commitment to yourself, a pledge to honor your needs and nurture your well-being. Embrace this commitment, and let it guide you toward a more balanced and fulfilling life. With self-care as your foundation, you are well-equipped to navigate the path ahead, ready to embrace the journey with confidence and grace.

"Healing may not be so much about getting better, as about letting go of everything that isn't you—all of the expectations, all of the beliefs—and becoming who you are."

Rachel Naomi Remen

CHAPTER TWELVE

Staying Motivated and Hopeful

Maintaining Motivation and Hope

"There is hope, even when your brain tells you there isn't."

John Green

I magine standing at the foot of a towering mountain, the summit hidden in the clouds. The journey upward seems daunting, but the path becomes more apparent as you take each step. This is often how it feels when managing anxious attachment and striving for emotional healing. The climb is steep, and sometimes you might slip, but you have the strength to carry on. In moments of doubt, remember this: "Hope is the whisper that says, 'Maybe, just

maybe, one step back doesn't mean you won't take two forward.'"
Hope is not merely an abstract concept but a powerful motivator
that fuels perseverance and resilience.

Maintaining motivation and hope can be challenging, especially
when faced with setbacks. It's easy to become overwhelmed by
the fear of failure or regression. However, it's essential to recognize that setbacks are not failures but growth opportunities. Every
step, even those taken backward, can teach valuable lessons.
When you learn from these experiences, you build a foundation
for future success. This mindset helps transform obstacles into
stepping stones, reinforcing your determination to keep moving forward. Embracing this perspective requires patience and
self-compassion, acknowledging that progress is not always linear
but often a series of ebbs and flows.

Cultivating hope involves nurturing a positive outlook and focusing on what is possible rather than dwelling on limitations.
This shift in perspective can be achieved through various practices, such as mindfulness and gratitude. Mindfulness encourages
you to stay present, observing your thoughts and feelings without judgment. This awareness helps prevent you from becoming
entangled in negative thought patterns. Gratitude, on the other
hand, shifts focus from what is lacking to what is abundant in
your life. Engaging in daily gratitude exercises can create a sense
of contentment and enhance overall well-being, reinforcing hope
and motivation.

Interactive Element: Gratitude Reflection Exercise

Take a moment to reflect on three things you are grateful for today. Write them down in your journal and why they matter to you. This exercise not only strengthens your sense of gratitude but also serves as a reminder of the positive aspects of your life. Revisit these entries when you need a boost of encouragement.

It's also important to share your aspirations and achievements with others. Doing so can create a network of support and encouragement, creating a sense of community. Sharing your journey with trusted friends or partners allows them to offer perspective and celebrate your successes. This communal aspect of motivation can be compelling, reminding you that you are not alone in your struggles. It reinforces the idea that, together, you can navigate the challenges of anxious attachment and emerge stronger on the other side.

The Role of Professional Help: Therapy and Beyond

The path to healing from anxious attachment can feel like navigating a complex maze, where professional support becomes a crucial guide. Seeking help from a therapist or counselor provides you with expert guidance, offering personalized strategies tailored to your unique experiences and challenges. Trained professionals can help you uncover and address underlying issues and traumas that might be difficult to confront alone. They bring a wealth of knowledge about effective interventions, such as Cognitive Behavioral Therapy (CBT) or psychodynamic approaches, each designed to help reframe your thoughts and improve your emotional responses. Group therapy and support groups offer a different kind of support, where sharing experiences with others facing similar challenges can allow for connection and understanding. In these settings, you gain insight not only from the facilitator but from the shared wisdom of the group. Coaching or counseling can also offer practical tools for growth and self-improvement, focusing on actionable steps to overcome obstacles.

Finding the right professional help requires thoughtful consideration. Start by researching therapists or coaches who specialize in attachment issues or anxiety. Look for qualifications, such as licensure and experience in relevant therapeutic methods. Building a trusting and collaborative relationship with your chosen professional is vital. This trust allows you to explore vulnerable topics and work together effectively. Set clear goals and expectations to ensure your sessions are focused and purposeful. Whether you wish to improve your emotional regulation, enhance relationship skills, or gain deeper self-awareness, clearly articulated objectives guide the therapeutic process.

To make the most of professional support, engage actively in your sessions. Approach each meeting openly and honestly, candidly sharing your thoughts and feelings to uncover deeper insights. Practicing and applying strategies learned in therapy outside of sessions is crucial, reinforcing new habits and coping mechanisms in your daily life. Regularly reviewing your progress with your therapist helps track improvements and identify areas that need further attention. This ongoing evaluation ensures that therapy aligns with your evolving needs and goals.

Therapy was my turning point. I am still seeing my therapist. My needs and goals may have shifted over the time I have seen her, but that is the best part; they kept evolving as I evolved and changed into sessions that were beneficial for me and where I am on my path. I am incredibly grateful for therapy and finding the right therapist who is there for me and, will never give up on me and keep helping me along my way. Remember, too, that every therapist is different, and don't be scared to find a different therapist if you feel like your sessions are not benefiting you. Think of it as a friendship or relationship; not everyone will get along, so don't be scared to find the right fit.

Your Journey Ahead: Embracing a Secure Future

Picture a life where you wake up each morning feeling confident and secure in your relationships. You communicate openly without the nagging fear of abandonment. Picture managing your emotions with grace, responding rather than reacting. This is what a secure and emotionally healthy future looks like. It's a place where you lead a fulfilling and balanced life, navigating both the joys and challenges with resilience and poise. To make this vision a reality, define your personal and relationship aspirations. Consider what you truly want—perhaps it's a harmonious partnership built on trust or a deeper understanding of yourself. Once you've identified these aspirations, create action plans to achieve them. Break down each goal into manageable steps, setting milestones to track your progress. This makes the goals more attainable and provides a clear path forward. Regularly review and adjust your goals as needed, allowing for flexibility as you grow and change.

This adaptability ensures your goals remain relevant and aligned with your evolving self.

Maintaining a growth mindset is crucial in this process. Embrace challenges as opportunities for growth rather than obstacles that hinder your progress. This mindset encourages resilience, encouraging you to learn from experiences rather than fearing failure. Stay open to new ideas, skills, and perspectives, continually seeking opportunities for self-improvement. Celebrate your ongoing progress and achievements, no matter how small they may seem. Recognize that each step forward is a testament to your dedication and strength. This positive reinforcement boosts your confidence and motivates you to keep moving forward. As you continue on this path, remember that growth is a lifelong journey, not a destination. There will always be new lessons to learn and new heights to reach. Embrace this journey with an open heart and a curious mind, knowing that each day brings a chance to improve yourself.

Celebrating Your Progress: Small Wins Matter

Recognizing and celebrating "small win" achievements is vital for maintaining motivation. Each small win reinforces positive behavior, creating momentum that propels you forward. These celebrations boost your self-esteem and confidence, as each acknowledgment reinforces a sense of accomplishment and progress. Celebrating these steps encourages continued effort and growth, reminding you that every little stride contributes to your larger goals.

There are various ways to celebrate your progress, each as unique as the journey itself. Keeping a "success journal" is a simple yet effective tool, where each entry documents an achievement, no matter how small. This journal becomes a tangible reminder of your progress, a testament to your resilience and dedication. Rewarding yourself with small treats or activities adds joy to the process. Whether it's a leisurely walk in the park, a new book, or a favorite meal, these rewards serve as milestones that mark your dedication. Sharing successes with supportive friends or partners can strengthen relationships and provide a network of encouragement. As you share your achievements, you invite others to celebrate with you, creating a sense of community and shared joy.

Tracking your progress is another crucial aspect of celebrating small wins. Progress tracking charts visually represent your accomplishments, allowing you to see how far you've come. Reflection prompts can guide you in assessing growth, offering insights into areas of strength and those needing more focus. Regular self-assessment check-ins provide a structured approach to evaluating progress, ensuring you remain aligned with your goals. These methods not only help in recognizing achievements but also in maintaining a sense of direction and purpose.

The impact of recognizing small wins extends far beyond the immediate satisfaction they bring. Each celebration builds confidence and self-efficacy, reinforcing your ability to achieve your goals. This creates a positive feedback loop, where each success fuels further motivation and effort. Consider Sophia, who rewarded herself with a spa day after reaching a personal milestone. This act of self-care reinforced her commitment to her goals, providing a moment of reflection and rejuvenation. Then there's Liam, who found strength in sharing his progress with a support group. He felt empowered and inspired to continue on his path through their encouragement. Imagine an individual celebrating milestones with friends and family, their collective joy creating memories that fuel future endeavors. These stories illustrate the profound impact of celebrating progress, highlighting how small wins contribute to long-term success.

"Consistency: It's the jewel worth wearing; It's the anchor worth weighing; It's the thread worth weaving; It's a battle worth winning."

Charles Swindoll

Real-Life Success Stories

There's something profoundly uplifting about hearing real-life stories of transformation. These tales of triumph over adversity breathe life into the abstract concepts of healing and change. They serve as beacons of hope, reminding you that the challenges of anxious attachment are not insurmountable. Hearing about others who have walked similar paths and emerged stronger can motivate and inspire. Such stories offer concrete proof that healing is possible and can ignite a spark of determination within you.

Consider the story of Alex. Once plagued by a deep-seated fear of abandonment, Alex's relationships were often chaotic. His need for constant reassurance created tension, driving wedges between him and his partners. However, Alex began to reshape his attachment style through consistent self-care and emotional regulation. He sought the support of a therapist, who guided him through techniques like cognitive restructuring and mindfulness. Over time, Alex developed a secure attachment style. His relationships transformed as he learned to trust both himself and others, creating connections built on mutual respect and understanding.

Then there's the story of Maya and Ben, a couple who found themselves in a cycle of conflict and miscommunication. Both struggled with anxious attachment, leading to frequent arguments and misunderstandings. Determined to rebuild their relationship, they committed to open communication and trust-building exercises. They attended couples therapy, where they learned to express their needs and fears without blame—by practicing patience and empathy, Maya and Ben rebuilt their bond, transforming their relationship into a supportive partnership. Their success embodies the power of collaboration and commitment to change.

These stories share several common elements. Consistency in practicing self-care and emotional regulation was pivotal. Both Alex and the couple prioritized their well-being, recognizing that change requires dedication. Seeking support from therapy and support groups provided guidance and accountability. Through these resources, they gained insights that nurtured growth. Persistence and resilience in the face of setbacks were also crucial. Each faced moments of doubt and challenge, yet they persevered, drawing strength from their progress.

Reflecting on your own journey can reveal your growth. Consider journaling as a tool to track personal development. Write about the moments that challenged you and how you overcame them. Reflect on the milestones you've reached, celebrating each achievement. By viewing your journey as a success story in progress, you cultivate a mindset of resilience and hope. This perspective allows you to see each step forward as a victory, no matter how small. Your path may be unique, but like Alex, Maya, and Ben, you can transform challenges into triumphs.

Conclusion

As you reach the end of this book, remember the primary purpose: to guide you in understanding and managing your anxious attachment style, building secure relationships, and creating lasting self-worth. The path to emotional healing and secure attachment is not a sprint but a marathon; every step you've taken is a testament to your commitment and courage.

Throughout the chapters, we've explored the core of anxious attachment, tracing its roots from childhood experiences to its manifestations in adult relationships. You've delved into the emotional landscape, learning to navigate intense feelings and identify triggers. Building self-awareness has been a crucial part of this journey, allowing you to understand your reactions and develop self-compassion. The practical exercises and strategies for healing, such as mindfulness, journaling, and emotional regulation techniques, are tools to carry with you beyond these pages.

We've discussed the importance of finding comfort within yourself, healing past wounds, and embracing holistic approaches like nutrition, physical activity, and creative expression. Communication emerged as a vital skill in nurturing and improving relationships, while strategies for transitioning to a secure attachment style offer a roadmap to a more stable and fulfilling life. Long-term strategies emphasize the importance of consistency and the power of a supportive network.

Key takeaways from this book include a deeper understanding of anxious attachment, recognizing and managing emotional triggers, and developing self-compassion. Practicing emotional regulation techniques and improving communication skills are essential steps toward healing. Transitioning to a secure attachment style is possible through persistent effort and holistic approaches that enhance overall well-being.

Ongoing practice is vital. Integrate these strategies into your daily life, and let them become part of your routine. Consistency will pave the way for lasting change. I encourage you to revisit the chapters and complete the exercises as you continue your journey. Set specific, achievable goals based on the strategies outlined. Engage actively and take proactive steps forward.

Remember, you're not alone. Many have walked this path, including me, and have emerged stronger and more secure. Your progress is significant, and the potential for a more fulfilling life is within reach. Embrace the journey with courage and compassion for yourself.

For further support, consider exploring additional resources. Books, websites, support groups, and therapy options can provide deeper understanding and guidance. Seek out what resonates with you and complements your healing journey.

Thank you for trusting me to accompany you on this path. Your courage and commitment to personal growth and healing are commendable. It has been an honor to contribute to your journey toward emotional well-being and secure relationships.

As you close this book, take a moment to reflect on the progress you've made. Each step, whether forward or backward, is a valuable lesson. Healing is a journey; every small achievement is a milestone toward a more secure and fulfilling life. Remember, a step back is not a failure but a lesson on how to proceed forward. You are capable of charging ahead with newfound strength and resilience. You've embarked on a transformative journey, and the future holds endless possibilities. Keep moving forward, and embrace the life you are creating for yourself. You got this!

Keeping the Journey Alive

Now that you have everything you need to build healthier relationships and feel more secure, it's time to share your newfound knowledge and show other readers where they can find the same help.

Simply by leaving your honest opinion of this book on Amazon, you'll show other people who are struggling with anxious attachment where they can find the information they're looking for and pass on their passion for healing and growth.

Thank you for your help. The journey toward secure attachment is kept alive when we pass on our knowledge - and you're helping me to do just that.

To make a difference, simply click the link below or scan the QR code and leave a review:

https://www.amazon.com/review/review-your-purchases/?asin=1966973012

Thank you from the bottom of my heart!
Angelina Peck

References

35 quotes about communication for inspiring team collaboration. (n.d.). https://vibe.us/blog/35-quotes-about-communication/?srsltid= AfmBOoqVKwgJz5qtkuKvLgTuM3fF249DacTUk-qQjArc4xU EW58_9pOV

Anxious attachment style in Relationships Complete Guide. (2023, December 8). Attachment Project. https://www.attachmentpr oject.com/anxious-attachment-relationships/

Bailee Boggess, M. (2024, June 9). *115 Relatable Quotes About Overthinking to Inspire Peacefulness and Letting Go.* Parade. Retrieved December 5, 2024, from https://parade.com/living/ overthinking-quotes

Basics of Nonviolent Communication – BAYNVC. (n.d.). https:// baynvc.org/basics-of-nonviolent-communication/

Blacher, S. (2023). Emotional Freedom Technique (EFT): Tap to relieve stress and burnout. *Journal of Interprofessional Education & Practice*, *30*, 100599. https://doi.org/10.1016/j.xjep.202 3.100599

Calm Editorial Team. (2024, February 8). *7 tips on how to communicate your needs in a relationship — Calm Blog.* Calm Blog.

https://www.calm.com/blog/how-to-communicate-your-ne
eds-in-a-relationship#:~:text=To%20express%20your%20n
eeds%20effectively,%22%20or%20%22I%20need.%22

Clinic, C. (2024, July 11). *How to start a Self-Care Routine.* Cleveland Clinic. https://health.clevelandclinic.org/how-to -start-a-self-care-routine

Collective, A. L. T. (2024, May 30). *Growth in Relationships: 5 Ways to Create a Growth-Oriented Relationship.* Anchor Light Therapy Collective. https://anchorlighttherapy.com/h ow-to-have-a-growth-oriented-relationship/

Drescher, A. (2024, January 23). *How to Move from Anxious Attachment to Secure.* Simply Psycholo- gy. https://www.simplypsychology.org/how-to-move-from -anxious-attachment-to-secure.html

Effa, C. (2023, September 26). *How can you fix an anxious attachment style?* https://www.medicalnewstoday.com/arti cles/how-to-fix-anxious-attachment-style

Fargo, S., & Fargo, S. (2024, March 12). *60 Healing Quotes that Inspire: A Journey to Inner Peace.* Mindfulness Exercises. https://mindfulnessexercises.com/healing-quotes/

Floyd-Douglas, A. (2024, November 19). *40 consistency quotes to help kickstart your future.* SUCCESS. https://www.success.com/consistency-quotes/#:~:text=%E2 %80%9CSuccess%20isn't%20always%20about,will%20com e.%E2%80%9D%20%E2%80%94Dwayne%20Johnson

Fountaine, K. (2023, August 3). *The Power of Rou- tines: 4 Ways Establishing Consistency Supports Men- tal Health - One Change group.* One Change

Group. https://onechangegroup.org/the-power-of-routines
-4-ways-establishing-consistency-supports-mental-health/

Fritscher, L. (2024, July 1). *Understanding fear of abandonment.* Verywell Mind. https://www.verywellmind.com/fear-of-abandonment-2671 741#:~:text=This%20fear%20can%20also%20cause,often%2 0the%20most%20effective%20option.

Gillette, H. (2022, February 28). *Fear of intimacy: when you are afraid of getting too close.* Psych Central. https://psychcentral.com/blog/afraid-of-getting-close -to-someone-fear-of-intimacy

Gotter, A. (2023, March 22). *8 Breathing exercises to try when you feel anxious.* Healthline. https://www.healthline.com/h ealth/breathing-exercises-for-anxiety

Groves, O. (2022a, June 9). *45 Journaling prompts for Healing.* Silk + Sonder. https://www.silkandsonder.com/blogs/news/35-journaling -prompts-for-healing?srsltid=AfmBOop_eV22vLy31ffeiH9s bqhnICf5Blt70pMbsAiRmfv35asveidI

Groves, O. (2022b, June 9). *45 Journaling prompts for Healing.* Silk + Sonder. https://www.silkandsonder.com/blogs/news/35-journaling -prompts-for-healing?srsltid=AfmBOop_eV22vLy31ffeiH9s bqhnICf5Blt70pMbsAiRmfv35asveidl

Gupta, S. (2023a, May 26). *The Importance of Self-Reflection: How looking inward can improve your Mental health.* Verywell Mind. https://www.verywellmind.com/self-reflection-i mportance-benefits-and-strategies-7500858

Gupta, S. (2023b, December 6). *Why trust matters in your relationship and how to build it.* Verywell Mind. https://www.verywellmind.com/how-to-build-trust-in-a-relationship-5207611

Gupta, S. (2024a, March 22). *25 Self-Love affirmations to remind you of your worth.* Verywell Mind. https://www.verywellmind.com/25-self-love-affirmations-8553223

Gupta, S. (2024b, April 18). *What does secure attachment look and feel like? plus how to develop it.* Verywell Mind. https://www.verywellmind.com/secure-attachment-signs-benefits-and-how-to-cultivate-it-8628802

Harper, C. (2023, June 22). How to build a support system for your mental health. *MyWellbeing.* https://mywellbeing.com/therapy-101/how-to-build-a-support-system

How We Healed an Anxious Attachment Style and Created More Security and Space in Our 12-Year Relationship: Deep Dive with the Solls [ep. 27] | mindspo.com. (2023, July 6). https://mindspo.com/2023/07/06/how-we-healed-an-anxious-attachment-style/

Jd. (2023, August 5). *21 Extraordinary Quotes that Will Change the Way You Treat People.* Sources of Insight. https://sourcesofinsight.com/quotes-that-will-change-the-way-you-treat-people/#:~:text=%E2%80%9CDo%20to%20others%20as%20you,that%20same%20treatment%20to%20others.

Jones, H. (2024, July 24). *What it means to have anxious attachment.* Verywell Health. https://www.verywellhealth.com/anxious-attachment-5204408

Lcsw-C, H. B. P. a. L. L. (2023, January 16). Emotional safety is critically necessary—and widely misunderstood. *Psychology Today*.

https://www.psychologytoday.com/us/blog/the-art-of-feeling/202301/emotional-safety-what-it-is-and-why-its-important

"Life isn't about waiting for the storm to pass. It's about learning how to dance in the rain." —Vivian Greene. (n.d.). The Foundation for a Better Life. https://www.passiton.com/inspirational-quotes/6501-life-isnt-about-waiting-for-the-storm-to-pass

Lpccmhc, K. R. M. (2022, March 10). It isn't comfortable, but it fosters communication and connection. *Psychology Today*. https://www.psychologytoday.com/us/blog/happy-healthy-relationships/202203/the-importance-of-vulnerability-in-healthy-relationships

Martin, L., Oepen, R., Bauer, K., Nottensteiner, A., Mergheim, K., Gruber, H., & Koch, S. C. (2018). Creative Arts Interventions for Stress Management and Prevention—A Systematic Review. *Behavioral Sciences*, *8*(2), 28. https://doi.org/10.3390/bs8020028

Mayo, L. (2024, May 7). *DEAR DIaRy: The benefits of keeping a journal*. https://www.linkedin.com/pulse/dear-diary-benefits-keeping-journal-luke-mayo-quyle

MFT, A. B. P. (2018, April 2). The healthiest response to childhood emotional wounds is also the rarest. . . *Psychology Today*. https://www.psychologytoday.com/us/blog/mindful-anger/201804/9-steps-healing-childhood-trauma-adult

MSc, O. G. (2024, March 6). *Anxious attachment style: What it looks like in adult relationships*. Simply Psychology. https://www.simplypsychology.org/anxious-attachment-style.html

MSEd, K. C. (2023, February 22). *What is attachment theory?* Verywell Mind. https://www.verywellmind.com/what-is-attachment-theory-2795337

Plata, M. (2018, October 4). How embracing routines can
positively impact your mental health. *Psychology Today*. https://www.psychologytoday.com/us/blog/the-gen-y-ps
y/201810/the-power-of-routines-in-your-mental-health

Plumptre, E. (2023, February 17). *Learning how to cope with relationship anxiety*. Verywell Mind. https://www.verywellmind.c
om/learning-how-to-cope-with-relationship-anxiety-5186885

PsyD, M. a. M. (2024, June 12). Recognizing our accomplishments
fuels motivation, growth, and success. *Psychology Today*.
https://www.psychologytoday.com/us/blog/empower-your-mi
nd/202406/from-small-steps-to-big-wins-the-importance-of
-celebrating

Psyjdc. (2018, January 6). *Improve Attachment
Style with Mindfulness*. Contemplative Stud-
ies. http://contemplative-studies.org/wp/index.php/2018/01/0
6/improve-attachment-style-with-mindfulness/

Raypole, C. (2024, January 29). *30 Grounding techniques to quiet
distressing thoughts*. Healthline. https://www.healthline.com/
health/grounding-techniques

Riopel, L. (2019, September 14). *17 Self-Awareness Activities and
Exercises (+Test)* (T. Sauber Millacci, Ed.). PositivePsychology.
Retrieved December 5, 2024, from https://positivepsychology
.com/self-awareness-exercises-activities-test/

River Oaks Psychology. (2023, October 9). *12 Proven
Trust-Building Exercises to repair relationships of all
types*. https://riveroakspsychology.com/12-proven-trust-buildi
ng-exercises-to-repair-relationships-of-all-types/

Robinson, L., Segal, J., PhD, & Smith, M., MA. (2024, October
23). The mental health benefits of exercise - HelpGuide.org.

HelpGuide.org. https://www.helpguide.org/wellness/fitness/the-mental-health-benefits-of-exercise

Schultz, J. (2020, September 24). *Forgiveness Therapy: 6+ Techniques to help clients Forgive* (J. Nash, Ed.). PositivePsychology. Retrieved December 5, 2024, from https://positivepsychology.com/forgiveness-in-therapy/

Self-Compassion. (2024a, September 24). *Self-Compassion practices: Cultivate inner peace and joy - Self-Compassion.* https://self-compassion.org/self-compassion-practices/

Self-Compassion. (2024b, November 10). *Self-Compassion by Kristin Neff: Join the community now.* https://self-compassion.org/

Selhub, E., MD. (2022, September 18). *Nutritional psychiatry: Your brain on food.* Harvard Health. https://www.health.harvard.edu/blog/nutritional-psychiatry-your-brain-on-food-201511168626

Suni, E., & Suni, E. (2024, March 26). *Mental health and sleep.* Sleep Foundation. https://www.sleepfoundation.org/mental-health

Sutton, J. (2022, October 8). *Inner Child Healing: 35 Practical Tools for Growing Beyond Your Past* (T. Sauber Millacci, Ed.). PositivePsychology. Retrieved December 5, 2024, from https://positivepsychology.com/inner-child-healing/

Team. (2024a, April 23). *How to Self-Soothe Anxious attachment Triggers - AP.* Attachment Project. https://www.attachmentproject.com/blog/self-regulation-anxious-attachment-triggers/

Team. (2024b, April 23). *How to Self-Soothe Anxious attachment Triggers - AP.* Attachment Project. https://www.attachmentproject.com/blog/self-regulation-anxious-attachment-triggers/

Understanding Anxious attachment | Relational Psych. (n.d.). https://www.relationalpsych.group/articles/understanding-anxious-attachment#:~:text=How%20can%20therapy%20help%20with,(EFT)%20are%20particularly%20effective.

Utah State University. (n.d.). *Using active listening to enhance your relationships*. USU. https://extension.usu.edu/relationships/faq/using-active-listening-to-enhance-your-relationships

Vinney, C., PhD. (2024, June 26). *The dating behaviors that trigger my anxious attachment style*. Verywell Mind. https://www.verywellmind.com/anxious-attachment-triggers-8664174